THE ARCHITECTURE OF LEADERSHIP

How Power, Vision, and Influence Are Designed

By Gevorg Grigoryan

The Architecture of Leadership:
How Power, Vision, and Influence Are Designed

ISBN Paperback: 979-8-89576-174-8
ISBN Hardback: 979-8-89576-173-1

Published by:

 AUTHORS on MISSION

Table of Contents

Introduction

Design begins with recognizing a need.
—**Charles Eames**

When I was seven years old, my father brought me to visit a construction site in our neighborhood. Men were pouring concrete where a brand-new apartment complex would be built. I observed them smoothing the surface with long instruments, checking that every section was perfectly straight and flat.

"Dad, why do they spend such a long time on something nobody will ever see?" I asked.

My father was a contractor and engineer. He pointed at the workers smoothing the concrete. "Because everything else depends on that part. If it fails, the whole building fails."

It made me rethink everything, not buildings, but life, business, and how to deal with people.

Years afterward, I established my own architectural practice. I learned that the very qualities that make buildings sturdy make leaders successful, too. Both require foresight. Both require groundwork. Both must be built incrementally, with extreme care given to every step.

Most books on leadership either mention personality types or management techniques. This book is different: it puts the design of effective leadership in the clear light of understanding, providing blueprints that effective leaders either consciously follow or unconsciously adopt.

I've planned houses, office buildings, and public spaces. I've also assembled teams, led projects out of the jaws of crisis, and enabled others to accomplish things they didn't believe were doable. These processes are very similar.

When you walk into a well-planned office, you know it instantly.

The rooms move well together.

Lighting illuminates the right spots.

Everything is where it is meant to be and has a purpose.

Effective leaders have a similar influence on teams and organizations. What many people do not understand about architecture is that the beauty lies within the underlying framework. The unseen parts determine overall visibility.

The same is true of leadership: planning, preparation, and the thoughtful development of systems; the intangibles produce the tangibles that everyone appreciates.

In these pages, you will learn to think architecturally when you lead. You will learn to draw blueprints of your vision. You will learn to build foundations that last. You will learn why some leadership architectures fall apart, and others endure across generations.

I wrote this for anyone who wants to lead better: students preparing for their first jobs, managers struggling with difficult teams, entrepreneurs building companies, parents raising children, and military officers developing strategy. The principles apply everywhere because human nature remains constant, just like the laws of physics that govern all buildings.

You don't have to know anything about architecture to profit from this book. I will explain everything simply. When I use technical terms, I will clarify their meanings and why they're important to your leadership.

My purpose is to provide you with techniques that apply on the ground, not theories or motivational addresses, but techniques that can be implemented today. These techniques have helped me design buildings that accommodate families, offices where individuals flourish, and a company that contributes to our society.

Architecture taught me that all great buildings start with vision. Then comes the blueprint. Then comes the foundation. Then comes the careful construction, piece by piece, of something beautiful and usable.

The same is possible with your leadership.

Watch me do it.

PART I

The Planning Phase

Every structure starts the same way, with nothing but space, potential, and nothingness. Before the first spade hits the earth, before the first wall can be constructed, before anything physical has been made, there has to be vision. There has to be planning. There has to be a detailed visualization so that something imagined can be created.

The same holds true for leadership.

In Part I, I share the process of developing the vision that launches everything that follows. I teach you how to think like an architect before the first brick has been laid, to envision what isn't there, to describe it in such a way that others can help create it, and to adopt the architect's mindset that means the difference between successful leaders and busy ones.

This is where it all begins. Learn this, and the rest will fall into place, and you'll save the trouble of cleaning up messes that existed before you started.

CHAPTER 1

Creating Your Leadership Vision

Imagination holds the power to rescue an idea.
—Frank Lloyd Wright

I was maybe seven years old when I first understood what leadership meant. My father told me a story about an employee who saw his boss driving a new Lamborghini. The employee said, "Hey, boss, that is a nice car. Very beautiful. I like it."

The boss looked at him and said, "If you continue to work as hard as you have, if you work days and nights, if you work overtime and deliver even better quality, then next year I'm going to buy my second car."

From that day on, I thought, I'm not going to buy a car for somebody else. Let me be the leader. Let me be the person buying my own cars. I'm going to be a leader everywhere.

Most people think leadership starts when you get promoted or someone puts you in charge. It's not like that. Leadership starts when you decide to create something better than what exists, when you see something wrong and think, "I can fix this," and when you look at a situation and know there's a different way to do it.

But wanting to lead and knowing how to lead are completely different things.

How Vision Works in Architecture

When clients come to my office, they typically begin by telling me what they do not want.

"I do not want it to look like my neighbor's home."
"I do not want tiny rooms."
"I do not want to pay a lot."

They think they are guiding me. In fact, they are misleading me.

A good architect helps clients move from knowing what they do not want to having a clear sense of what they do want. We must clarify clients' vague suggestions and provide substance. We must show them what their prospective homes will look like before we lay the first brick.

A similar pitfall must be avoided with leadership vision. Most prospective leaders are aware of the type of leader they do not wish to be: the yelling boss, the micromanager, the one who takes credit for others' work.

But knowing what you do not want doesn't reveal what you wish to build.

My Two Dreams that Became One

I had two separate dreams for my life, and for a long time, I believed they were two different things.

My initial dream was to become a leader. After hearing the Lamborghini story, I knew I wanted to be the one who made decisions. I wanted to create something of my own.

My second dream was to create and to draw. As far back as grade school, I drew anime-style pictures and sold them to other students. I loved painting and drawing, and I also loved math. I sold my drawings as a grade school kid, and to this day, I am still selling my drawings.

When I got older, I realized these aren't two different dreams. They are the same dream from different angles. The love for creating and the desire to lead both come from the same place. Both come from seeing something that could be better and having the confidence to make it happen.

When I found architecture, it all fell into place. I enjoy doing business, and I enjoy drawing. The combination of these two passions is what architecture is all about.

Leadership works the same way. You need creativity to see new solutions. You need practical thinking to make them work. You need to understand people and systems.

From Idea to Real Plan

In architecture, the first phase is called "programming." That's when we figure out what the building needs to accomplish. How many people will use it? What activities will happen inside it? What's the budget? What are the site restrictions?

You might design the most beautiful building in the world, but without solving problems during the programming phase, it's useless.

Leadership vision works the same way. Before you can lead anyone anywhere, you need to know where you're going and why. You need to understand what problems you're trying to solve.

I've learned that most people skip this step. They jump straight to tactics. They start making decisions before they understand what they're trying to accomplish.

When I started NextGen Vision with $500 in my pocket, I did not have a business plan. I did not have an office or any hardware, but I did have something better than both of those things: I knew what I wanted to create.

I wanted to create an architectural firm that was all about family, where architects could come not just to learn but to develop; where we would create beautiful things to enhance people's lives, and where success would be measured not only by revenue but also by relationships built.

That vision drove every choice I made, even when I printed work at a copy shop because I couldn't afford a plotter of my own.

Getting Others to See What You See

The hardest part of architectural design isn't designing the structure; it's how to tell clients what you're showing them.

When you show somebody a blueprint, they see lines on a sheet of paper. They cannot necessarily imagine how the rooms will look or how sunlight will move through the building throughout the day.

That's why we develop 3D visualizations and virtual tours, to help others see the dream before it comes to life.

Leadership vision suffers when you see the future you are building, but others do not. You must help people envision the direction you are heading and why it is important.

I learned this early on in practice. I'd be enthusiastic about a project and launch into the details. The clients' eyes would glaze over. They were not interested in structural engineering or codes. They simply wanted to know how their families would use the rooms and navigate the space.

I began to weave narratives instead: "When you wake up in the mornings, you'll walk from your bedroom to the kitchen, and you'll see sunlight streaming through this big window. In the evenings, your children will sit at the kitchen island doing their homework while you cook dinner, and you can talk to them the entire time."

Suddenly, they could see it. They could feel it.

The same thing happens with leadership vision. Don't talk about management philosophy. Talk about the future of what you want to create. Help people see how what they do on a daily basis is connected to the big picture.

Making Dreams Work in Reality

All design projects are founded on big ideas. Owners want it all: the biggest spaces, the best finishes, the newest technology. They want it fast, and they want it cheap.

That's part of the job: to preserve the vision but make it feasible. I have to find ways to provide clients with what they need, even if I cannot give them everything they want.

Other architects simply say "no" to clients who demand too much. That's not leadership. Leadership is discovering innovative solutions that advance the vision while accounting for real constraints.

Recently, we had a project that was neither small nor particularly large. When we looked at the architectural drawings, it seemed typical, but nobody understood what it was supposed to be. Even I, as the architect, found it difficult to interpret the plans when viewed from a client's perspective.

I looked at the project and asked my project manager:

"What do you think? Will the client like this project?"

"Why not? It is so beautiful."

"You see that it's beautiful," I responded, "but the client will not see it that way."

I added, "Okay, so let's do a detailed design for this. I know it's not included in the price, but let's do it on our end. Let's show it to him so he gets an idea of what's going to be there. If we show him just a plan, he might not be happy and could say, 'Oh, I don't like it. Do another drawing.' But I can see how beautiful that drawing looks."

So, funded out of my own pocket, we completed additional design work—specifically exterior design—so the client could understand the project. We did it, and the client loved the result. He said that when he first looked at the project, he hadn't imagined the place could be so beautiful.

Visionary leadership needs equal balance. You need big visions to motivate people to move forward. But you also need to translate those visions into steps people can take.

When I tell my staff we are going to be the best architectural firm in Glendale, that's the big picture. But I have to outline the specific projects we'll undertake, the skills we'll develop, and the systems we'll establish to get there.

The Foundation Everything Builds On

When I am building a house, the foundation is always the biggest component of the project timeline and expenditure. It frustrates clients at times because there is simply no progress for weeks.

But I tell them: it all comes down to this part being done correctly. If we do a quick foundation, we'll pay for it later in cracked walls, misaligned doors, and costly repairs.

Leadership vision is your foundation. You might be hungry to begin, make things happen, and get results. But if you do not take time to develop a crisp, inspiring vision that anyone can understand and can get behind, everything you build on it will be shaky.

The good thing is that once your vision has a solid foundation, everything gets simpler. Decisions are sharper because you have a standard for making decisions. People are more dedicated because they know what they are doing and why. Difficulties become doable because you know what you are aiming for.

Ever since I chose to be the one buying my own cars, rather than the one whose work helped buy someone else's cars, I've been learning how to turn visions into realities.

Now I have a company with 12 computers, 12 drafters, project managers, and a marketing team. We've won awards for four consecutive years. More importantly, we've created a place where people want to work and grow.

But it began with leadership vision, the belief that there is a better way, and wanting to create it.

Your leadership begins the same way.

CHAPTER 2

The Blueprint Mindset

Most creations change between the drawing board and reality. —**Maya Lin**

You know what I always use as an example?

In the army, they use large maps to plan and strategize military operations. I always compare those maps to an architect's blueprints. The contractor builds according to those plans, moving forward step by step.

Leadership and architectural discipline are connected. You can't be a good leader without architectural discipline. You need to have your plans in front of you: what you want to accomplish, how you want to lead your company, and how you will guide the people who are looking to you.

This is what I call "blueprint thinking." We associate blueprints with technical drawings of buildings, but blueprints are ways of thinking, ways of defining what's in your mind so clearly that somebody could build it according to the way you conceived of it.

Why Leaders Need Maps

When army generals plan military operations, they don't just say, "Let's go attack that city." They spread a big map on the table. They study the terrain. They mark where enemy forces are positioned. They plan multiple routes. They identify supply lines. They prepare for what happens if Plan A doesn't work.

Then they take that map and show it to all the commanders under them. Everyone looks at the same map. Everyone understands the mission. Everyone knows their part. When the operation starts, each unit can make decisions independently because they all understand the bigger plan.

That's a blueprint mindset.

Without the map, it's chaos. Men run off in all directions. Units attack the wrong targets. People get lost. There is goodwill but no coordination.

The same applies to a business, any company, or any group of people trying to do something together. You will not have a well-defined plan visible to everyone if people are expected to develop it along the way. They may move quickly, but in the wrong direction.

The Blueprint on the Table

If you move without a plan, you will never know how to proceed.

As in architecture and construction, if you don't have plans specifying how large the foundation needs to be for a specific location, and you proceed as usual—for instance, by using less than 2,500 PSI concrete—it might not be sufficient, or it might be more than necessary. If it's more than what you need, you'll spend too much money, but if it's not enough, the house could collapse.

So you have to have a plan. You must perform the calculations so you can start to build your house. In leadership, you need a plan that shows what you want, where to start, where you want to go, and how much money you need to achieve it.

If you don't have a plan, you're going to fail in your business and your future. You're going to fail everywhere. You'll be disappointed and say, "Okay, that's enough for me. I'm not a leader. I'm just a follower. So, I'm going to follow another leader." You'll just quit.

But you'll succeed if you have a leadership plan. Anyone can be a leader with their mental blueprints in front of them.

Making Ideas Real Through Documentation

When I started NextGen Vision, I had dreams of what I wanted the company to be. I had it all planned out in my mind: the office, the group of people working together, the things we would create, and how we'd engage with clients.

But when I tried to share my dreams with others, they failed to see what I was seeing. My ideas were too abstract.

That's when I learned an important lesson: if you can't draw it, you can't build it.

We have a process in architecture that turns abstract concepts into tangible forms. We begin with sketches, which are preliminary drawings that capture the basic idea. Next comes design development, where we create detailed drawings showing how spaces relate to one another. Finally, we produce construction documents, which are precise blueprints outlining every detail a contractor needs to build what we designed.

Leadership is no different. You begin with vision, the big picture of what you want to build. Next comes strategy, which is how the various pieces interconnect. Then you develop detailed plans: the specific actions people can take to bring the vision to life.

Most leaders bypass the intermediate steps. They begin with a wonderful vision and instruct people on what to do. But without blueprint thinking, the details do not connect to the vision. People strive to understand but do not know why. People do as they are instructed, but struggle to adapt once things are different.

When Planning Saves Everything

Let me tell you a story about a project where detailed planning saved us from disaster.

We were designing an addition. The client wanted to add a second story with a master bedroom and bathroom. It looked simple on paper, building up rather than out.

But when we went to do the measurements, I told my team, "Look, this is a project in Glendale, and in Glendale, these points are very important. So make sure to test everything and take all the measurements accurately."

We measured twice. We checked the foundation. We evaluated soil conditions. We studied how the structure was initially constructed. We documented all the details.

It was fortunate that we did. In reviewing all of the measurements, we found the foundation wasn't sturdy enough to hold the second story. The initial contractor had done a substandard job. Had we embarked on the construction without planning, the entire house might have fallen.

We developed a solution by reinforcing the foundation first, then adding an addition. It was a lot more expensive than the couple initially budgeted, but it was safe. Today, the house still stands, and the family enjoys having a new master bedroom.

That's what happens when you have a blueprint mindset. You see problems before they become disasters. You plan solutions before you need them. You build things that last because you took time to understand what you're building on.

The Military Map in Business

We hold weekly project management meetings in my company. I lay out all of our ongoing projects, just like those army generals and their maps.

We look at where each project is on the timeline. We identify what resources each project needs. We identify potential conflicts or delays. We plan for contingencies if the client changes their mind or if a permit is delayed.

Everyone on the team looks at the same information. Everyone understands how their work connects to the bigger picture. When problems come up, and they always do, people can make good decisions because they understand the overall plan.

For example, if authorization for Project A runs two weeks behind, and that releases us to move David, one of our managers, for two weeks, we can shift him to Project B and get it back on schedule. No one needs to wait for me to do anything because anyone can consult the map.

This is a blueprint mindset in action; not just having a plan, but making the plan visible to everyone who needs to execute it.

Making Abstract Ideas Concrete

One of my clients presented an extremely abstract concept. He told me, "I'd like a home that'll feel like home." It's a pleasant idea, but how do you create it?

I asked him questions. "When you think about feeling at home, what specific things make you feel that way? Is it gathering with family? Is it a quiet space for reading? Is it a view of the garden?"

Slowly, we turned "feels like home" into specific spaces and features—a family room where everyone can be together but still enjoy their own activities; a kitchen island where kids can do homework while parents cook; reading nooks by the window; a private patio for morning coffee.

Each abstract feeling became a concrete space. Each concrete space became a detailed drawing. Each detailed drawing became instructions for the builders.

The same principle applies to leadership objectives. "I want an engaged team" is vague. But "I want a team where people don't mind sharing ideas, where people comprehend how what they do helps the company succeed, and where people help one another if issues come up" is detailed enough to work with.

Afterward, you can create tailored practices: weekly team meetings in which each member contributes one idea; monthly presentations in which each person explains how their ongoing project supports the company vision; and a buddy program in which seasoned employees guide new workers.

Abstract becomes concrete. Concrete becomes actionable. Actionable becomes real.

Building Plans Others Can Follow

When I sketch a building, I am not sketching a structure I can build. I am drawing a structure others can build, knowing I will not be present to supervise every move.

The blueprints have to be so clear that a contractor who has never met me can look at them and understand exactly what I want. The electrical drawings have to be so detailed that the electrician knows where every outlet goes. The structural plans have to be so precise that engineers can approve them without asking questions.

That's the test of a good blueprint: Can it be used by somebody to create what you imagined?

Plans for the leadership require equal clarity. If you are sick for a week, can your group still move forward? If someone departs from the company, can another person replace them and do what they did? If a new person joins the group, can they look at your systems and know what to do?

True leaders do not make themselves indispensable by involving themselves in every decision. Instead, they focus on building systems that function without them.

When Plans Need to Change

What's key to a blueprint mentality: Having a plan does not imply that the plan will not be altered. Even on a building site, we occasionally must adjust drawings if we find anything unexpected.

But when you have a good plan, changes are controlled and intentional. You don't just start to build something different. You change the drawings first. You make sure the changes are consistent with the rest. You announce the changes to all.

Same for leadership. You adapt plans, but shifts are intentional and openly communicated. You do not change course for convenience. You analyze why your plan is not producing. You create a new method. You refine your "blueprints" and present them to your people.

A blueprint mentality does not require adherence to the initial plan, but it does require having a clear plan at any given time so that when you do change direction, people have something to follow and won't get lost.

Your Leadership Blueprint

If you want to develop a blueprint mindset, start with these practices:

- Document your vision in writing. If you can't explain it clearly enough for someone else to understand, it's not clear enough for you to execute.
- Break big goals into smaller, specific actions. Each action should be concrete enough that anyone could do it if necessary.
- Create systems for regular review and adjustment. Set times to look at your plans, assess progress, and make necessary changes.
- Share your plans with others. The people who execute the plan should understand not only what to do but also why they're doing it.
- Plan for problems before they happen. Ask yourself: What could go wrong? How would we respond? What backup options do we have?

Remember: The goal is to be so well prepared that you can adapt quickly when the future surprises you.

Just like those army generals with their maps, great leaders always have their blueprints ready. They know where they're going, how they plan to get there, and what they'll do when obstacles appear.

The blueprint is your leadership map. Without it, you're just wandering around hoping you'll accidentally end up somewhere good.

PART II

The Construction Phase

Plans are beautiful things. Visions can be inspiring. Blueprints look great in theory.

But none of that matters until you start building.

This is where the work of leadership translates from theory into reality. This is where you lay the groundwork upon which the rest of your work will be built. This is where you lead the people doing the day-to-day work. This is where you set up the systems by which everything else hums along. And this is where you learn to adjust your plans when reality bites.

This is the tough part. This is where most leaders fail, not because their vision is flawed but because they don't understand how to develop it. I will demonstrate the construction process.

CHAPTER 3

Building Strong Foundations

True liberty rises from the inside.
—Frank Lloyd Wright

In Russia, in 2015, I observed a three-story building crumble in less than one minute.

The contractors had tried to save money on the foundation. They thought nobody would notice, so why spend extra? They paid off the inspector and used concrete that wasn't strong enough for what they were building.

The foundation looked fine from the outside. The first floor went up without problems. The second floor, same thing. By the third floor, everyone thought they had gotten away with it.

Then one afternoon, the workers began running. They just threw down their tools and ran. All three stories collapsed within a second or two, as if someone had yanked a plug. Dust was everywhere. Steel beams were twisted. Everything they worked on for three months turned to rubble because they had attempted to skimp on the part nobody was supposed to see.

That's what happens when your foundation fails. It doesn't matter how beautiful the upper floors are. It doesn't matter how much work you put into the details. If the base isn't solid, everything falls.

The same is true with leadership. You can have the best strategy, the sharpest people, and the sharpest ideas, but if you're not building on foundations that have depth, you're going to see everything disintegrate.

What Remains When All Else Changes

My team is like another family to me. That's a non-negotiable.

To truly fit in on my team, it helps to feel like part of the family. I strive to create an environment where everyone feels they belong.

People think I'm being soft when I say this. They think "family" means we sit around having nice conversations, and nobody ever receives constructive criticism. That's not what I mean at all.

Family means when you make a mistake, I don't throw you away. Family means I teach you how to fix things. Family means your success matters to me as much as my own success. Family means I protect you even when it costs me.

A few years ago, we were growing very fast. We hired a lot of new employees in a short time. Then I started to notice the team was divided. The older employees, meaning the ones who had been with us the longest, were on one side. The newer employees were on the other side. There was a fight between them.

I knew the employees who had been with us longer. They understood we were family, and they were not causing the division. So I started looking for who was responsible.

Within 15 minutes, I dismissed six workers.

They all knew me. They all knew it was less hassle for me to hire somebody than to fire them. It was very hard, but I had to do it. Otherwise, we would have lost the company—the thing that we created, the way we did things, and the reasons people wanted to be part of it.

Those six individuals were good workers. They understood architecture. They could prepare plans and communicate with customers. They, however, broke the foundation. They taught newcomers that it was all about competition, not cooperation. They led by bad example, trying to move ahead by pulling others down rather than strengthening the team.

I could not let that concrete harden. Once that sort of thinking is ingrained in your foundation, it cannot be eradicated. It will eventually tear everything apart.

The Second Load-Bearing Wall

No one is to speak negatively to my team, including customers.

Sometimes I can understand why a customer is frustrated or angry. Projects do not go as planned. Permits take longer than anyone anticipated. Fees are higher than expected. I get it.

However, when they speak to my employees, their tone should always be calm and respectful.

One time, while working with a regular customer, one of our team members helped with a task that was outside the scope of work. However, we did it because we valued the client; he had numerous projects for us, and we wanted to keep him satisfied.

The team member came back to the office, and I could tell that she was not happy. She was angry. I asked, "What is happening? Something has happened, hasn't it?"

She told me that the man had started shouting at her and slammed the phone down.

So I called him. This customer had given me substantial work, sent us steady business, and probably accounted for the majority of our income for the year.

But I cared more about my team than the projects.

I confronted him.

"Listen, if you feel the need to speak harshly or raise your voice at anyone on our team, direct it at me, not them. The others are my employees, and they are under my protection. If you want to yell at anyone, yell at me. Then see if you can."

He apologized. We continued to collaborate. But he never yelled at anyone on my team again.

Some might argue that I jeopardized the retention of a high-paying client due to one phone call. They might say I should have spoken to the employee, informed her that clients get stressed, and educated her on how to deal with difficult people effectively.

People who might say these things do not comprehend foundations. If I had let that client's behavior slide, I would have shown everyone in my office that their dignity is less important than money, that I protect them only up to a certain point, and that I will only do so much to stand up for them.

That's not a foundation that holds weight. That's the kind of base that looks fine until pressure is applied, and then it cracks.

What You Refuse to Bend On

The third non-negotiable is the list of prices.

I have discounts. I could offer you a discount. However, I have a minimum amount I will not go below. These days, many people offer their services at lower prices, but this often leads to lower quality and less respect for the work itself.

It is better to lose a job than do it too cheaply.

Our studio begins work for a minimum of $4,500. I will not accept less than that.

Once, I had a friend who was working on a small project; a couple of hours of work, perhaps. He was my friend, so I felt I could not ask him for $4,500.

I thought to myself, "I am going to do it for free."

I worked on the project. When he asked me how much he would have to pay, I said it would cost him nothing. He said, "That's not possible. You did the work."

I told him, "Listen, my minimum price is too costly for this project. So it is better to do it for free instead of breaking my price list."

People do not understand this. They think I am stubborn or hard-headed. They say, "Just charge him $2,000; it is better than nothing."

They're wrong, though. When you bend your own rules for convenience, rules become recommendations. And recommendations do not support buildings or businesses.

When you stick to your rules and sell your work for what it's worth, you uphold your integrity and standards. If you're willing to compromise that for a few 1000 dollars, what else might you compromise when the pressure is even greater?

The price list can be a foundation issue. It's crucial to mean what you say.

When the Ground Cannot Bear You Up

You don't always discover foundation issues while building.

We once had a project at a home with an existing garage. The work involved converting spaces, adding rooms, and making several improvements. During the architectural phase, we didn't anticipate any issues with the current structure. The paperwork was in order, the square footage matched the records, and everything appeared legal and correct.

Then we received the permits to start construction. We had to add to the foundation to enlarge the house. We excavated along the walls to connect the new foundation to the old one.

We observed that the house itself lacked support. It is just resting on a slab.

If we put anything on it, the entire house would be pulled down. The distribution of weight would all be wrong. The slab would crack. Everything would fail.

We had to redo the entire project: the architectural drawings, the engineering calculations, and the building plans. We had to lay the foundation for the original house first, since it was sitting on a slab like a box on a table.

It took much longer than expected. It created extra work for us. But we saved the project. We added the foundation first, then continued construction.

The customer was dissatisfied with the delay and the additional expense. But I clarified: "You could spend this money now to do it right, or you could spend a lot more money down the road when your house starts to develop cracks and your addition begins to detach from the rest of the structure. It's your choice."

They did it right. The house still stands. You would never know that part of it was added; it all appears to have been originally built that way. You can't see that there was ever an issue.

That is what good foundations do. When they're working properly, they go unnoticed, but everything relies on them being in place.

The Infrastructure Nobody Sees

In construction, infrastructure refers to systems that render a building habitable but that its occupants often do not perceive, such as electrical wiring in the walls, plumbing pipes in the floors, ventilation ducts in the ceilings, and load-bearing beams within the framing.

Leadership uses a similar infrastructure. Trust is the wiring that conducts communication throughout your team. Respect is the piping that ensures relationships flow cleanly. Principles are the supporting beams that uphold every decision that you make.

When I say no one is to speak disrespectfully to my team, I am not being defensive. I am building infrastructure. Each time I stand up for someone, I add another link to the trust system. Each time a team member observes me accepting accountability for a misstep, they discover that they, too, may own up to their mistakes without being punished.

One of my workers once told me something that I never imagined I would hear from anyone. He said, "Gevorg, I like working for you. You never make mistakes."

I didn't comprehend it initially. Making mistakes from time to time is human. All of us make mistakes.

So he clarified. He noted that when someone makes a mistake, I do not point it out to them. Instead, I say, "This is not your fault. That is my fault because I failed to show it to you."

I wasn't trying to make a point or prove anything. I was simply being honest. If someone on my team doesn't understand how to do something, that's my responsibility. I'm the one who recruited them, the one who was supposed to help them develop their skills, and the one who assigned them to a job they weren't yet ready for.

But that honest response created infrastructure. It built a system where people don't hide their mistakes. They bring them to me immediately because they know we'll fix them together rather than arguing over whose fault it is.

That is the infrastructure that enables everything else to happen. We're able to move more quickly because individuals won't hesitate to do things in a new way. We're able to undertake larger projects because team members ask questions rather than act as if they know something when they don't. We're able to grow because inexperienced workers observe experienced workers and aspire to do it that way too.

It all stems from foundation-level decisions about how we treat each other.

What You Build That Lasts After You're Gone

The proof is when something stands on its own and doesn't falter once you stop supporting it.

I've educated David and Eva, my managers, in everything I do: each technique, each method, and each solution. When others ask if I am concerned that David and Eva might depart to form their own companies, I answer honestly: that's my risk to manage and not their risk to avoid.

I've considered it another way. I could maintain certain secrets to make myself indispensable, but then I would have to be involved in everything indefinitely. If I were the bottleneck, the organization could expand only to the extent that I allowed it.

Alternatively, I could train everyone to be as competent as I am, perhaps even more skilled in certain areas, and hope that they would simply wish to stay.

I chose the second option. Now, I completely trust David and Eva. I call them to ask how projects are going. Everyone on the team takes responsibility for all tasks, because nothing is reserved for me alone.

That's a foundation that will outlast me. If something happens to me tomorrow, NextGen Vision won't fall apart. The systems will keep running. The standards will stay the same. The culture will continue.

Most leaders put themselves at the center of all processes because it makes them feel significant. They become the core, rather than establishing one within the organization. When they leave, everything falls apart, because it all depends on their presence.

I wanted to build something else, something in which principles constitute the foundation, not the person who built them.

My team is family. That's the first beam. Nobody talks badly to my team. That's the second beam. We don't break our standards for convenience. That's the third beam. Together, those three principles hold a lot of weight.

They sustained the weight of firing six individuals in one day when it would have been simpler to turn a blind eye to the issue. They sustained the weight of confronting a valuable customer when it would have been more financially beneficial to overlook the conflict. They sustained the weight of refusing less profitable projects when we were in need of money.

Those beams are still holding. They'll keep holding after I'm gone.

Because that's what actual foundations do. They don't just support what you're building today. They support what you're building for years and decades to come.

They're likely still cleaning up rubble from the structure that collapsed in Russia. Maybe they rebuilt it from scratch. Maybe they gave up. However, I guarantee you this: if they had to do it all over again, they would invest more money and time in the foundation.

Some things you only learn the hard way. However, you don't necessarily need to do it the hard way. You can look at the rubble and decide to do it better from the start.

These aren't just theories of leadership, but the actual beams that support everything else. They involve decisions that may seem insignificant until you see your entire structure built upon them.

Your foundation is being built right now, whether you know it or not. The question is whether you're building it sturdy enough to support what you want to create.

CHAPTER 4

Raising the Walls: Framing Your Leadership Structure

When solving a problem, beauty isn't my focus—but if the final answer lacks it, something is off.
—Buckminster Fuller

My friend purchased property and wanted to put in some retaining walls. It was a small job, not too involved. First, we conducted the soil test, as we normally would, to determine what kind of foundation we would need.

We got the report, and we all just stood and stared at it, baffled.

The whole area was filled with dirt. When we dug down looking for actual soil, there was nothing—just filler material, going down and down. We had to spend substantially more time and money to excavate until we reached native soil.

The weird thing is, his house had been sitting there for years, since the 1950s, on compacted dirt. I don't know who allowed that. I don't know why the house hadn't fallen. But when we went to expand it, we couldn't just build on top of the existing structure. We had to dig deeper, through all that false ground, until we could find something solid.

That is what it means to test the site in architecture. You cannot simply stand on the surface and presume that you know what lies beneath. You must test. You must dig. You must determine what you are building on before building your walls.

That is also the case for leadership. You enter what appears to be a solid relationship, and only discover when you're in the process of building that it is not built from the ground up.

What You're Actually Looking At

When I first interview a new client, I'm really not listening to what they say they want.

That sounds bad, but it's true. Everyone says they want something cheap, fast, and beautiful. They want more space but don't want to spend money. They want a traditional style but also modern features. They want everything done yesterday, but also done perfectly.

If I followed only their words, I would create the opposite of what I should. Instead, I seek to understand the meaning of the words and what the client truly desires.

Recently, someone approached us and stated that they desired a brand-new unit in the rear yard. Just a second unit, an accessory dwelling unit (ADU), for income from rentals.

I went to the site, and I said, "Listen, you've got your main residence, and you want a new unit. Why don't we do three brand-new units?"

The client was taken aback initially. He hadn't thought of that. But I clarified: "You're doing it for business, right? You don't need it as an additional residence. You will lease it and derive income from it. When you sell your house, you can also sell the rear unit as a duplex. So if you're investing, let's invest more."

That's what I do when I "read the room." I look past what people think they want and try to see more deeply into what they need. And I show them the best way to do it.

This was an individual seeking passive income. He didn't necessarily want just one ADU, but that was all he could think of. When I mentioned that he could have three on the same piece of land and receive three times the rental income, his entire mindset suddenly changed.

I'm always looking for the best options, the highest value, and the most significant returns. My goal isn't to make more money from clients, but to ensure they get the most for the money they're already spending.

Interpretation Between the Lines

The most difficult projects to estimate are those where the customer does not know the real problem.

If they claim they want more space, I could sketch an addition, collect my fee, and move on. But if I ask enough questions, I may discover, for example, that their existing layout requires the entire family to march through the kitchen just to get anywhere. They don't want more square footage. They want improved flow.

Another scenario: They want to knock down a wall and have an open floor plan like the homes they see on television. However, when I arrive at the house, I notice that the wall is load-bearing, and tearing it down would cost three times their budget. So I may recommend another configuration that would open up the space without causing a structural disaster.

This is why an architect is not just somebody who sketches houses. It is easy to put lines on paper. But can you anticipate what a client needs before they know they need it? Can you spot issues that they do not even know they have? Can you see the situation clearly enough to direct the client toward the best solution, even if it differs from the original request?

In leadership, this skill is essential. Your team members will not always inform you of the actual problem. An employee may complain about having too much work when, in reality, the issue is that they do not understand the project's purpose. Another may request different software when, in fact, they simply need more training on the current software.

If you listen only to what is said, you will only ever scratch the surface of core issues. You must know how to interpret ground conditions, how to test the soil, so to speak, beyond the surface.

The Structure That Nobody Planned For

We once had a project in which we conducted all the typical evaluations. We observed the property lines, assessed the setback specifications, and confirmed the zoning. Everything was in order.

Then, when we began working, we found the property line was not aligned with the fence. The fence had been standing for years, and everybody thought it was on the property line. When we conducted the proper survey, we found the neighbor's fence extended three feet onto my client's property.

That threw everything off kilter. Suddenly, our planned addition no longer made sense. We had to redo the entire layout to include actual property lines rather than assumed ones.

Nobody was trying to deceive anybody. That fence had been standing for so long that people assumed it marked the property line. Assumptions, though, do not change facts. That property line was a fact, regardless of what anyone assumed.

I observe the same thing in firms all the time. Someone works for a team and questions why they do things a certain way. The firm responds, "Because that's the way we've always done them." Nobody knows why, or whether the reasons are still pertinent.

It's like that fence; it looks like a boundary, so people think it's a boundary. However, the reality is different. If you're going to build something that lasts, you've got to know the difference between what is real and what people just think is real.

When the Ground Isn't What It Seems

The retaining wall project revealed an insight into assessment. We could have simply designed the walls based on the average conditions of the soil. We could have determined that the average foundation depth called for standard reinforcements and provided plans that would have been accepted and approved.

Then, during construction, everything would have failed. The walls would have leaned, cracked, or collapsed because they were built on fill dirt instead of real soil. And everyone would have blamed the contractor, the engineer, or the designer.

But it would not have been their fault. It would have been my fault, for I failed to see the actual conditions before formulating the remedy.

That's the result when you sidestep the observation phase. You develop solutions for the idealized world you imagine, not the world as it is. And you're surprised when things don't go as planned.

With leadership, plans that sound perfect in a planning session may not work in practice. For instance, you may create an incentive program based on your assumptions about what motivates your team, without asking your team members what motivates them. You may reorganize reporting relationships according to an organizational chart, but without understanding those working relationships and communication processes.

You build on fill dirt and wonder why nothing stays standing.

The Weight Distribution Problem

Framing in construction is more than constructing walls. It involves placing weight in the right places so that the structure can resist the loads intended for it.

If you place all your weight on one beam, it collapses. If you do not account for lateral forces such as wind or earthquakes, your building sways back and forth until it fails. If you do not securely fasten parts, you may have strong individual components but an overall weak structure.

The same is true for organizational structure. You shouldn't have all the most important information in one person's mind. You shouldn't subject all decisions to one approval point. You shouldn't have siloed departments with minimal interconnection.

So when I started NextGen Vision, I was the frame. All projects went through me. All clients went through me. All tech decisions went through me. That was fine when we were small, but when we scaled, I became the failure point.

So I had to reorganize. I had to distribute the workload among multiple individuals. David and Eva now make tech decisions that I used to make. Client relationships are the responsibility of project managers. Issues get fixed without involving me.

That was not simple to build. It involved teaching others what I had previously kept for myself. It involved acknowledging the possibility that they might do things in ways I would not personally do them. It involved relinquishing control over tasks I had previously managed.

Now the structure can support more weight, since I am not the only support system.

Building Up Without Falling Down

What they don't tell you about growth: the higher you build, the more precise you need to be with your supports.

A single-story building is more forgiving of imperfections. The loads are relatively small. The forces are manageable. You have some room for error.

But when you start adding stories, everything changes. Small mistakes made at the start get magnified. Mild angles become major alignment issues. Weight that might be reasonably distributed across one story becomes unsafe when you multiply it by the number of stories.

I've seen companies try to expand in the same ways they did when they were small. They keep the same decision-making model. They keep the same casual communication and systems.

Then they wonder why everything is confusing, why problems never get resolved, and why individual aspects of the company do not work in tandem.

It's because they didn't reframe when they built up. They just kept adding more weight to a building that was never designed to bear it.

The Philosophy of Yes

People ask me if, when NextGen Vision was gaining momentum, I ever experienced a period when I had to slow down or avoid expanding too rapidly.

The answer is no.

I never say no to opportunities. I don't like to go backwards. I always take forward steps.

One of our workers says I taught her never to decline an opportunity. Any project is an opportunity. We say yes, and then we make it work.

Anything is achievable with teamwork.

But I had to use the utmost caution. Remember when I had to terminate six workers in 15 minutes? It was when what we were building risked collapse, and I had to act fast.

We were growing quickly: new projects, new customers, and new additions to the team. It was all going up. However, I could see the team was dividing, with longtime employees on one side and newer employees on the other. It was competition instead of cooperation, politics instead of partnership.

That is a structural issue, not a problem with the organization's culture, but rather a framing problem. The organization's configuration was actually causing stress in the wrong places. The seasoned employees weren't integrating the new hires into the existing framework; instead, they were building separate structures alongside it.

Had I allowed that to continue, we would have ended up with one building housing two companies. Something would have inevitably cracked: the old team would have left, the new team would have been pushed out, or the whole thing would have split in two.

So I didn't slow down growth. I fixed the frame. I removed the elements that were creating the structural problem, and I reinforced the connections between the parts that remained.

Then we continued to expand. But the building remained strong because everyone was operating within the same structure, supporting the weight together rather than pulling in opposite directions.

What Assessment Actually Is

When designers assess a site, we don't just look at today's conditions. We consider the future.

Can this property accommodate two stories, or will the soil conditions call for expensive foundation work? Is this site big enough for what the client wants, or will they need to make do with less? Does the neighborhood require us to complement existing architectural styles, or can we design something more contemporary?

We read limitations and opportunities simultaneously. Each limitation indicates what could be improved. Each problem points us to an innovative solution.

That was what I was doing when I informed my client that he could pursue a three-unit project instead of just one unit. I wasn't simply trying to increase the project's scope; I was assessing what could actually fit on his property, what would comply with zoning regulations, and what aligned with his ultimate objectives. My goal was to show him how to make the best use of all these factors together.

Others see only the limitations. They look at a small lot and think, "few options." They see complicated zoning and think "circumscribed alternatives." They see a low budget and think, "not much we can do."

Constraints, however, provide a valuable outline. They show the boundaries so that you may decide what's optimal.

When I look at a project or team, I ask the same things: What is the real potential here? What do we need to avoid? What is feasible that hasn't yet been conceived? Where do we have solid footing, and where do we have fill dirt?

The Part You Can't See Yet

That is the essence of framing: it doesn't look like much at first, just wood beams and studs without any walls, finishes, or other features to make it look pretty. When potential homebuyers see a job site, they wonder, "That's all? We're paying for that?"

However, your framing determines everything that follows. The size of each room, the placement of doors and windows, the height of the ceilings—all these choices depend on the underlying framework.

It doesn't make sense to focus on perfect finishes if you haven't gotten the underlying framework right. If the structure is flawed, you'll end up with rooms that don't feel right, awkward traffic paths, and spaces that simply don't work well.

Leadership framing is the same. The organizational structure you build determines how information flows, how decisions get made, how quickly you respond to problems, and how well different functions work together.

Everything else will fall into place if you get that structure correct. But if you do it wrong, you will end up spending years undoing issues ingrained in your structure.

That is why evaluation is so important. You cannot construct the correct scaffolding if you do not know what you're building on, what forces you're working with, and what you're aiming for.

So, before you put up walls, before you make fundamental structural decisions, before you spend money on an end result that will be expensive and difficult to alter, test everything. Dig all the way down. Find the actual property lines. Test the ground to see what it will bear.

Then create a structure that can support what you intend to place on it.

CHAPTER 5

Leading the Build: Managing Your Construction Crew

Dyslexia taught me that voices insisting something can't be done rarely matter, so I don't treat refusal as final. —**Richard Rogers**

I walked into the office one morning and announced we had a new project. The owner had built everything back when the old California codes allowed it, but the area had since been downzoned. He could no longer build that big, but he still wanted to add a little more.

Everyone was claiming it was impossible. We can't do that. The codes won't allow it. No way.

I told my team, "All right, $100 goes to whoever can come up with a workaround, because I already informed the client that we can do the project."

Everyone began searching through the codes, researching everything, attempting to discover a means by which we might make this possible. But this was one of those projects where you had to think outside the box. There are usually ways to bypass requirements if you know where to look.

The team pushed themselves to present answers to me. I kept saying, "No, that's against the law. We can't do that part. That's not going to work either."

Then someone approached me and asked, "Gav, I don't know, maybe I'm going to sound completely ridiculous, but might this code do it?"

I said, "Good job. You thought outside the box, and you found it. The $100 is yours."

That's how I lead projects. I always try to keep my team engaged with challenging tasks. I support them from the side, but I make sure they can handle the work themselves. One of my main goals is to help the team grow, not just myself. So when the next challenge arises, they won't depend on me; they'll be able to find solutions and succeed on their own.

Standing to the Side While Standing Behind Them

Just last month, we had a job where we encountered something no one would have ever expected. When we started, everything was fine. The house had been built some time back, and we needed to add a significant addition. Simple enough.

Then, when we began working on the drawings and blueprints, we discovered that the main sewer line for the entire area ran directly beneath the foundation of the existing house. We were planning an addition, but the sewer line ran beneath the foundation. Most architects would contact the client to apologize and explain that the project couldn't proceed.

But I would never tell a client it can't be done. We were going to find a way to do it, and I trusted my team to resolve it.

That's the main point. Whenever I participate in a project, I do so from the sidelines. I give everything to my two managers. I give them tasks to figure out for themselves.

Ultimately, I help them, but even when I step in, I do so from the sidelines, allowing them to see that they accomplished it themselves. That way, it's clear they were the ones who succeeded, not me.

This is unlike most leadership, which typically involves a total takeover or abandoning people to sort things out themselves. I'm doing something different. I'm with them, rather than in front of them. I'm next to them, sometimes behind them, so that I can give them what they need. But they're the ones who end up sorting it out.

When that team member anxiously presented me with his "stupid" idea for the code, I might have responded with, "Yes, I already knew that, but I was waiting for you to discover it." Then it would have become my solution. However, he's the one who thought outside the box and developed it. I already knew the answer, but that's irrelevant. He's the one who looked until he found it.

That is leading from the side. You know the answer, most likely, but you allow others to be the ones to arrive at it.

The Morning That Sets Everything

My typical day starts with a cup of coffee.

When I enter the office, the team is sometimes already busy with their coffee. Sometimes I invite everyone to go outside with their coffee and discuss projects. On those mornings, we discuss ongoing projects: where we are, what we're doing, and what's left to do.

After that, everyone heads to their computers and begins working. I review the projects, the team works on new assignments, and the managers coordinate with those responsible for each task.

This might sound casual, almost too relaxed. But this coffee time is where most of the actual leadership happens. It's not formal meetings with agendas and PowerPoints. It's standing around with coffee, talking through each project.

Someone says a permit is running longer than planned. We discuss whether to follow up or whether it's within standard timing. Someone reports that a client is inquiring about relocating a window. We determine whether that impacts the structure or is a straightforward change. Someone asks for advice on detailing a particular connection. We settle it amongst ourselves.

By the time we are seated at our desks, everybody knows what they are doing and why it is important. They know which projects are priorities. They know who needs help with what. They know I am available should something arise.

Coffee is more than coffee. It's your daily site meeting, your check-in, and your team alignment, all occurring under circumstances that feel more natural.

When I Step in Directly

I was involved in a project where, at one point, I noticed that the plan checker started working against us. This happens fairly often, since some city plan checkers are also architects. They can be difficult, especially when they see you growing as a competitor in the same city.

I do not work in a single city; I take on projects throughout California, including neighboring towns around Glendale. Some plan checkers who are also architects can't take on projects within their own city, but they can in neighboring cities, making them competitors there.

Sometimes, a plan checker might make things harder for you in the city where they work, which can affect your reputation in other cities.

When dealing with the city or a plan checker, I take charge when things become challenging or confrontational. I don't go to the city to fight, but I do stand my ground and explain when a plan checker is being unfair or acting with bias against me.

Every fight is mine.

My team doesn't have to worry about politics. They don't need to concern themselves with personal animosities or career jealousies that occasionally arise. They can focus on performing well. When that performance is questioned on matters unrelated to quality, that's when I intervene.

This is part of leading from the side. I am not in control of all the specifics of every project. However, I always look for the points at which my involvement can make a difference in the outcome. These are points where my experience, authority, or willingness to have tough conversations can insulate the team and keep projects going.

The Things that No One Observes

Prior to employing managers, I turned architects into managers. Whereas I previously conducted quality inspections, the managers now handle this task. But when I did it myself, I was rather finicky.

The lines on paper matter. Even if I fit three different drawings on a single page, I always balance them to make the composition beautiful. The plans should look appealing on paper. Even if the owner doesn't understand them, when another architect sees them, they'll say, "That's beautiful."

That's one aspect. Another is my approach to the plans themselves.

For instance, I don't like unnecessary corners or hallways. You can't have a house without any corners, but the fewer, the better. I always say that corners are where dust collects. When someone cleans the house, it's much harder to clean the corners than the straight areas. So, the fewer corners there are, the less dust will accumulate and the cleaner the home will be.

As for hallways, I often point out that nobody really uses them; they're just spaces to walk through. Yet the homeowner pays property taxes on that square footage without actually using it. I like to ensure that every penny the homeowner spends is for space they can truly use. It is impossible to have no hallways, but we can make do with as few as possible.

Each detail must be smooth. The flow of movement, how a person walks through the house, should also be exceptionally smooth.

I once told one of my employees, "When someone moves through this area, they'll have to turn their leg awkwardly. This corner will collect dust; we don't even need it. Instead of building the wall this way, we can make it straight, eliminating the corner and the dust."

She responded, "What are you saying? Do we really need to consider how people will clean or whether they have to walk carefully?"

I explained, "No one will notice you considering these things. But if you don't consider them, everyone will complain that the architect didn't think about their needs. Attention to detail often goes unnoticed when done right, but its absence is always felt."

When I conduct a quality check, I consider the person who will live there: How will they move through the house? How will they keep it clean? How will they keep it warm in winter or cool in summer? Every single detail matters toward quality of life in the home.

Quality control is more than just looking at measurements and making sure walls are plumb. That's part of it, but it's primarily about whether someone's everyday life will be improved because of your decisions. It ensures that clients pay property taxes on spaces they actually use, that they can negotiate corners when cleaning, and that they can walk through the space effortlessly.

If the architecture is obtrusive, something isn't right, but if the client lives comfortably without even noticing the architecture, you've succeeded.

The Writer and the Reader

Once, we created a very beautiful exterior design for a modern house. We carefully concealed the gutters that carry rainwater from the roof, because we didn't want to use ordinary, visible gutters. The hidden gutters complemented the modern aesthetic, and the owner specifically requested this design, which we were able to achieve.

But when I reached the construction site, I realized that the contractor did not know how to execute the vision.

I said, "You are the contractor. I am the architect. My drawings are like a book; I am the writer of that book, and you are the reader. If you skip pages, you will not learn anything. But if you read every page, you will understand the book and fall in love with it."

I added, "The drawings show how the gutters should be covered, but if you missed those details, how would you know how to construct them?"

He responded, "Okay, can we fix them without hiding them?"

I said, "No. This is a unique project with a specific design that we want to keep beautiful. If the gutters are visible, the result won't be as beautiful as I intended or worked for. The owner paid me for my time and effort, and now that work is being compromised. You're wasting the owner's money, even though he already paid me. You need to fix this and give the gutters the proper look."

He was a little sad. The next day, he tried to talk to the owner, telling him we could do it another way that would be easier. He pushed his idea.

I went back to the site. The owner called me and said, "You know, the contractor mentioned something very fascinating, and I believe we can attempt it."

I said, "Look, I designed this house. Even if you like it after talking with the contractor and making those changes, I won't like it. Because everyone who comes to your house, all your guests, will ask who the architect was. And I want you to tell them, 'Gevorg was the architect. Gevorg was the designer. NextGen Vision made my project, and I am proud of it."

I continued, "If you tell people that this is the work of NextGen Vision, then it needs to be perfect. It needs to be beautiful and unique. I've put my time in. You paid me to make it beautiful. You've seen those pictures, that design, those renderings. You want it to be like that, right?"

I asked, "Now, imagine gutters going down from here. How would you like that? Would that be beautiful?"

Then I said something he did not anticipate. "Even if you agree, I won't permit it. Because my name is on that house. And my name is worth more to me than anything on earth."

I didn't want him to believe I was being obstinate or childish. So I explained, "I assure you that I am on your side, not that I just want to have my way. I want you to see that the design is good for you. You already approved and paid for it. Respect your money and your time."

I laid it out clearly, "You've spent time and money on this project and paid me for my work. I've dedicated time and effort to create this design for you. Now, because a contractor was careless, didn't read the blueprints properly, and took shortcuts, the end result has been compromised. I can't accept that. Tell him to fix it. I'll make sure he does."

The contractor was disappointed, but he did what we needed.

Some people said I was being stubborn, that I should have compromised, especially since the client seemed willing to accept the mistake, and that my insistence on aesthetics was causing delays.

But they don't understand what real leadership on a building site means. The contractor was testing whether the drawings were merely guidelines or requirements, and the client was being persuaded to settle for less than what he paid for. If I had allowed that to happen, everything else would have become negotiable. The contractor would have kept finding "easier" ways to cut corners, and in the end, the project would have suffered from one compromise after another.

My role wasn't simply to draw the plans. It was to ensure those plans became a reality, and that involved holding fast to the details that mattered most, even when it would have been easier to compromise.

What Gets Measured Gets Built Right

In construction, people say: "Trust, but verify." Trust that your builders will do a good job, but verify that by checking things.

I do the same with my team, except I verify differently. I'm not checking to catch mistakes. I'm checking to teach.

When I grade a design and see that it has too many corners, I don't simply give it a bad grade. I describe why corners are important. I encourage the designer to consider how corners affect housekeeping tasks. I explain it to them so that they can see it.

The next time, they plan with fewer corners. They now know how to think that way themselves.

If I see that someone has designed a long hallway, I don't say, "Hey, you should do it right." I say, "What is the owner paying annually in property taxes for that hallway? What are they getting for their money?" I leave it up to them. I want them to figure it out for themselves that it means charging clients for unoccupied space.

This approach is slower than simply pointing out mistakes and telling people to correct them. But that's not our goal. We aim to develop professionals who care as much as I do, who notice what I notice, and who think the way I think.

That's why you implement strong quality control systems, so you don't have to inspect everything yourself. Instead, you teach your team to inspect their own work.

The Projects that Test All Things

Regarding the sewer line issue I mentioned earlier, we resolved it. It involved weeks of research conducted by my managers, consultations with civil engineers, meetings with city officials, and innovative thinking about the rearrangement of system approaches. I was on standby, ready when needed, but allowing my team to be the owners of the resolution.

When they finally came to me with the solution, they beamed with pride. They had accomplished something they'd felt was impossible when they started. They demonstrated to themselves that they can solve tough issues without my intervention.

That was more valuable than any remedy I might have provided them personally.

That downzone assignment with the $100 wager taught the entire office that "impossible" is almost always "we don't know the answer yet." When a challenging task arises, instead of declaring it impossible, ask people to research how it might be possible.

The hidden gutters job taught the contractor that our plans aren't recommendations. The next time he works with us, he'll read the plans more carefully. He'll mind the details from day one rather than seeking ways to expedite things.

Every project teaches you something, not only about construction or architecture, but about the way we work, what we stand for, and what we are willing to fight for.

Where Work Truly Takes Place

Everybody thinks leadership happens in monumental moments—the speeches, the big moves, the dramatic interventions.

But leadership happens in the morning over coffee while discussing what everyone is working on. It happens when you present someone with a dilemma and want them to come up with a resolution. It happens when you review a drawing and demonstrate why corners are important to someone who will be cleaning.

It occurs when you allow your crew to receive credit for finding a fix for that pesky sewer line, despite having led them through it step by step. It occurs when you deal with disputes with tough city officials, so that your crew can be busy with good work rather than badgering bureaucratic officials to give you what you need. It occurs when you stand on a worksite and won't budge on a detail because your name is on the design.

The construction crew comprises not only those on the site wearing hard hats. It includes the drafters at desks, the permitting coordinators who manage projects, and the crew huddled over coffee in the morning, trying to determine what can be accomplished that day.

Leading a team means knowing when to intervene and when to hold back, when to instruct and when to leave things alone, when to confront and when to let someone else figure it out.

That's why you pay attention to corners, hallways, and hidden gutters. Those details reflect respect for the people who will live in the home as well as the money and time invested in the project.

The goal is to develop a team capable of solving even the most difficult problems, not by solving them yourself, but by training your team to approach challenges the way you do.

That's what it means to lead a build. It's not just about overseeing tasks, checking boxes, or staying on schedule and budget, though all of that is important. It's about cultivating people who can create beautiful things without your direct involvement, while you remain on the sidelines to support them if needed.

When a project is finished, and everyone is satisfied with the result, your team should feel that they were the ones who made it happen.

Because they did.

CHAPTER 6

Installing the Systems: Building Operational Excellence

Learning never really ends.

—Norman Foster

The house appeared complete on the outside; a gorgeous modern design with clean lines, precisely what the client wanted. When the owners went to settle in, however, things didn't work.

The lights wouldn't turn on in half of the bedrooms. The water pressure was incorrect. The air conditioner cycled continuously but failed to cool the house effectively. Each system had been installed by contractors who hadn't worked with one another.

The building contractor had brought in outside specialists for individual systems. The electrician worked without conferring with the HVAC man. The plumber set up pipes wherever it was easiest, without considering what other tradesmen needed. Each did their own job, but no one ensured that the jobs meshed as part of a whole.

We had to rip through walls they'd finished not even a few weeks earlier. We had to rework incorrectly installed systems. We spent another three months getting that house's intangible elements to actually do what they were supposed to do.

The client was angry. "Why did no one consider this earlier?"

That's the right question. Systems don't happen by accident. Someone has to design them, install them, test them, and make sure they work together. Most people focus on what's visible: the walls, the finishes, the design. But what makes a house livable is what you can't see.

Leadership is exactly the same.

What No One Notices Until It Shatters

In construction, we have what I call "unwritten rules." These are practices that everyone in the industry knows and follows, even though they're not in the official building codes.

Take electrical wiring, for example. Once the drywall goes up, you can't see the wires anymore. But there's a specific way that experienced electricians run wiring through walls. They follow consistent patterns: specific outlet heights and predictable cable paths. Because of these unwritten standards, other contractors can often locate wires without even scanning the walls.

This matters because the electrical system is the most critical system in a house. Everything runs on electricity. If a wire is damaged during construction, the entire system may fail.

Plumbing follows similar unwritten rules. There are practices that everyone knows and uses, even though they're not written in code. The patterns work for the same reason: consistency makes the system reliable. Plumbing is essential for maintaining personal hygiene, keeping the house clean, and ensuring access to potable water.

Now consider the HVAC system, or what we call "mechanical" in the industry. There are fewer unwritten rules about HVAC placement because the system is mostly in the attic, where everything is visible. But it's still crucial that all the ducts are installed properly and that the air return system works correctly with the supply system. If any of these components isn't properly considered, the system won't heat or cool the space effectively.

These are the systems within a building that enable its most essential functions. You can have the prettiest house in the world, but without a proper electrical system, you sit in the dark. If your plumbing isn't functioning, you can't use your kitchen or bathrooms. If your HVAC system isn't functioning well, you won't feel comfortable no matter how good your furniture is.

It's the same principle in business. You can have bright people with good intentions and a clear vision, but without proper support systems, your efforts will suffer.

Communication is the electrical wiring of an organization. It transmits information to where it needs to go. When communication systems are functioning well, people know what they need to know, decisions get made, and issues get resolved. When communication fails, nobody knows what anyone else is doing, and people work with incorrect information or no information at all.

Processes are the plumbing. They determine how work flows through the company. When they're well-designed, projects move from step to step without bottlenecks. When they're poorly designed, everything clogs up or leaks out and gets lost.

Culture is the HVAC system. It determines whether the work environment feels comfortable. When the company culture is strong, people want to be there. They produce their best work. When it's bad, people feel uncomfortable and look for the door, even when everything else is okay.

The Morning Coffee Wire

Remember when I told you my typical day starts with coffee? Sometimes my team makes the coffee, and sometimes I make it. We go outside, have coffee, and talk about projects.

That's not only a good habit. That's a communication system that I set up intentionally.

When I began NextGen Vision, I conducted formal meetings. People would sit down, review lists, write down action items, and follow up on them. It felt more like work. People were reserved in terms of what they discussed. They held back until it was their time to speak. Substantive information wasn't shared unless it aligned with meeting agendas.

So I switched it up. Rather than having more formal, planned meetings, we have coffee together in the mornings. It's relaxed; it's cozy; and people talk about what's really on their minds. Someone brings up an issue about a permit. Another says that they bumped up against the same issue last month and explains how they fixed it. Someone else asks for advice on a detail about a project. We figure it out on the spot.

By the time we get to our computers, everyone already knows what everyone else is up to. They know where the challenges lie. They know who needs help. Information has traveled to the right destinations, but informally rather than formally.

That's a system. It seems like simply having coffee, but it's really the electrical wiring that keeps the entire office connected and up to date.

Protective System for the Team

Each fight is my own. I mentioned that above, but I can elaborate on why this is a system rather than just a personality trait.

When I first started handling multiple cities, my team members would sometimes get stuck dealing with difficult plan checkers. They'd spend hours trying to navigate political situations they didn't understand. They were good architects, wasting time on fights instead of doing good work.

I realized I needed a system to handle this. So I created a rule: whenever there's an issue with the city or a plan checker, when there is a need to explain that something is wrong or that someone is acting against us, that responsibility automatically comes to me.

Nobody on my team has to decide whether to fight or back down. Nobody has to figure out the politics. They simply redirect those situations to me, and I handle them.

Another type of situation I handle directly is when clients disrespect my team. I already mentioned how I responded when a valuable client spoke badly to one of my employees. I didn't care that he was a paying customer. I don't allow anyone to talk down to my team.

Another example of an instance in which I assist directly is when a client signed our agreement without reading the timelines. We clearly outlined when deliverables would be ready, but she was impatient. She started calling two or three times a day, asking, "Where are we with my project?"

I told my employee to transfer her calls to me. When she called again, I asked, "Did you read the contract? Did you see the timelines?"

I explained clearly, "Every time you call us asking where we are, it adds another day to the timeline. When you call, we have to stop working to talk to you. Then we have to spend time remembering where we left off before we can continue your project. So don't call us again until the date on the contract when the preliminary design is due. I might start your project today, or I might start it the day before the deadline. That's not your problem. That's my problem. But I will have it on time."

This is like having a surge protector on your electrical system. When there's a power surge that could damage your equipment, the surge protector absorbs it before it reaches anything valuable. The equipment is my team: valuable people performing critical work. The surges are political battles with plan checkers, disrespectful clients, and unreasonable demands. I am the system that absorbs those surges so my team can keep working without disruption.

Building Quality Automatics

When I didn't have managers, I monitored each project personally. I was pedantic; even the paper lines had to be exact. I visualized each corner, each hallway, and who would be using it.

But that wasn't a system. It was me doing everything. The company was only capable of producing as much quality as I was individually capable of reviewing.

So I promoted some of my architects to managers. But I didn't just give people promotions and tell them to check quality. I taught them exactly what to look for and why it matters.

I never sat them down for formal lessons. I simply did the quality checks on their projects while they watched. Gradually, I noticed I was no longer giving them any corrections. That's when I told them, "Now you'll do quality pre-checks, and then I'll do the final check."

One day, I remember walking into the office and hearing Eva explain everything to another employee during a pre-check, using exactly my words, my reasoning, and my approach. That was the day I told David and Eva, "You're the ones who will do the quality checks now."

The quality system now functions without my scrutinizing each individual project. The managers consider corners, hallways, walking flow, and all the other factors I consider. They know to factor in the people who will clean the house, pay property taxes, and occupy the space.

I created a system that made my standards become their standards. Quality is maintained even without my personal inspection of the output.

That's like having a well-designed heating and cooling system installed in your house. The desired temperature is set and regulated mechanically. There is no need to keep adjusting it manually.

The Challenge System

Code challenges are routine. When we encounter a tough issue, I present it to the team as a challenge. Sometimes there's a monetary incentive, other times the reward is simply recognition. But it's always the same drill: "We've got an 'impossible' problem here, but I think you can figure it out. Go solve it."

This system performs many tasks simultaneously. It promotes problem-solving skills in my team. It keeps people from depending on me for answers. It makes them feel more confident, since they prove to themselves that they can handle the hard stuff. It creates a culture in which "impossible" means simply "we haven't solved it yet."

Almost every year, there are new updates to building codes. When I see the updates, I don't just present them to my team. Instead, I present them with a challenge: "This thing is possible now. How can we do it?"

Recently, there was a code update that allows much larger ADUs than had previously been permitted, but the path to executing these types of projects is tricky. I presented it as a challenge, and at first, my team couldn't figure out how to take advantage of the larger allowable size.

Any updates bring new challenges.

I involve myself from the side. I give the team challenges to solve for themselves. In the end, I help them, but I do so from the side so they can see that they made it, that they could do it.

This is a capacity development system within the organization. It is similar to a plumbing system that provides water to all supply points in a home. The challenge system provides problem-solving capacity to all points within a team.

When Systems Work Without You

The ultimate test of whether you've created systems rather than habits is what happens when you're not there.

Before, when I went on trips, I stayed connected with the company day and night. I visit Armenia often, and when it's day here, it's night there, and vice versa. My phone was always on, so I could always be reached. My laptop was always with me, so I could log in to my computer and handle things.

But now the whole team knows they can just talk to David or Eva. Problems get solved the same way I would solve them because they're now the experts modeled after me. The only exception is the protection issues, the political battles I handle. For those, I tell the team to give me the person's number, and I'll call them; otherwise, they can wait until I'm back.

That did not happen by luck. I had to train them in everything I know systematically. I had to develop processes so that they would be able to make decisions without me. I had to develop a system that ensures the company functions whether I am present or not.

Leaders who claim to desire a similar system seldom build structures that would enable it. They retain significant information for themselves. They insist on being part of every decision. They form dependencies rather than structures.

The Information Flow Problem

Initially, I was the one meeting all the clients, hearing what they wanted, and discussing projects with them.

Then I'd come back to the office and explain everything to David or Eva. It was taking twice the time. I started bringing one or the other of them with me to meet clients so they could hear everything firsthand and start projects themselves.

Now, when a client calls the office, the receptionist doesn't even transfer the call to me. She connects them directly with David or Eva because she knows they will meet with the client and understand the project. Following the same example, David and Eva don't attend client meetings together. Instead, each of them goes separately and brings another employee along, so that the employee can learn how to start a project and see it through to completion.

In a house, when electrical wiring is not properly planned, certain rooms receive power while others do not. The flow of information in a firm is no different. If you fail to plan the flow of information, some individuals receive what they need, while others are left guessing.

Our morning coffee system ensures daily coordination. But we also have formal meetings once or twice a month. These aren't like meetings in the movies, though. They happen during lunch. On those days, I tell everyone lunch is on me. We set up a spread on our meeting table that includes lots of food, like a birthday party, with barbecue, salads, and everything. We eat first, and only afterwards do we go through the projects.

I never do "official" meetings like in the movies because I don't want my team to feel like I don't trust them. I want them to feel that I'm one of them, like an older brother. At home, when something happens, you talk about it during dinner or when everyone's gathered together. There's nothing formal about it.

These aren't just meetings. They're the planned pathways for information to flow where it needs to go. They're the organizational wiring diagram.

When Systems Fail

I remember the time my server was hacked. I don't know who did it, but all the projects we'd been working on for the previous three years were deleted. I wasn't at the office. David called me and said they couldn't work because the projects were gone. I told him, "Okay, I'm on my way to the office."

Everyone was panicking. In situations like that, it's really hard to keep calm. I didn't say so to anyone, but at first I thought one of the employees had done it. But I couldn't understand why, because I'd never mistreated anyone. I started investigating, but everyone was in the clear. Nobody on my team had done it. It was truly a hack, and nobody at my firm knew anything about it.

What they also didn't know was that we had a backup server. I'd already invested in data protection and, thank God, could easily restore everything.

Building failures are instantaneous. The lights won't turn on. The water won't run. The house is either too cold or too warm. You immediately know that something is wrong.

System failures are harder to identify in organizations. Projects take too long without anyone understanding why. Information gets lost when people assume that someone else gets it. Mistakes happen again and again due to the absence of a system that can prevent them.

The key is to see patterns. If a problem persists, it's not a people problem. It's a system problem. Something is not working.

Building Systems That Last

The processes I've developed at NextGen Vision—the morning coffees, the challenge mode for addressing problems, the quality checks that managers perform, the automatic forwarding of political battles to me—will endure even when I am gone.

The morning coffee meetings will still happen. New problems brought up will remain tasks for the team to solve. Quality will still be checked in the same ways. Political matters will continue to be taken up with whoever is in my place.

That's what good systems do. They become part of the way things are done, independent of any particular individual.

What's the system I'm proudest to have created, the one I'm certain will still be in place 20 years from now at NextGen Vision, even if I'm no longer around? It's the trust: the way we stand for each other, and the family we've built.

We build easy maintenance into architectural designs. Plumbing leaks can be swiftly detected and repaired. The circuit breaker can be replaced without rewiring the house. Walls won't be damaged if the HVAC unit requires service.

Systems of leadership are no different. They are of the same caliber. New people can learn them, but they can also be modified as circumstances might dictate. They are robust enough to keep functioning even after people leave.

The Invisible Infrastructure

Do you remember that home I mentioned earlier, the one with the combined systems that did not communicate with one another?

We finally solved it. We redesigned how the systems interfaced. We ensured that the electrical, plumbing, and HVAC systems were integrated into a cohesive infrastructure rather than treated as three separate projects.

When we completed it, the house looked no different. There was no difference in the walls, ceilings, or finishes. But everything worked. The lights came on when the switches were flipped. The water pressure was regulated. The temperature was comfortable in every room.

The client no longer had to think about the house and could simply live in it. That's exactly the point.

Good systems are invisible when they perform well. You don't think about electrical wiring when you flip a light switch. You don't think about plumbing pipes when you turn on a faucet. You don't think about HVAC ducts when the air feels comfortable in your home.

The same holds for organizational systems. When communication systems are working well, people simply know what they are supposed to know. When process systems are working well, projects simply flow smoothly. When culture systems are working well, people simply enjoy going to work.

You don't see systems when things go the way they should.

My intention was to create infrastructure for NextGen Vision that nobody would need to think about. Employees come in, have a cup of coffee, discuss projects, do fantastic work, collectively fix problems, maintain high quality, take care of one another, and go home feeling good about the work they deliver.

That is all a result of systems I deliberately designed and implemented. But ask the majority of people in the office, and they would say it's because we simply have a good company culture and get along as colleagues.

They wouldn't realize they're describing infrastructure.

Installing Your Own Systems

If you are going to create a culture of operational excellence, you must shift from management considerations to infrastructure considerations.

Do not simply communicate; create communication systems. How will information travel? What are regular touch points? How will individuals know what they must know?

Do not merely defer; design delegation systems. What can others determine without you? How will others feel empowered? What is the protocol when people are unsure?

Do not simply impose quality; create quality systems. How will standards be upheld? What checks are performed by whom? How do people know what "good" is?

Do not simply create culture; design culture systems. How are your values enacted daily? What behaviors are rewarded? How are new people educated?

If someone came to me for advice on developing better systems in their company, here's what I'd tell them: Create a family. When you build a real family culture, you won't need to create anything else. Everyone in that family will naturally start creating what's good for the family.

This is what underlies everything else. You can have vision, strategy, great people, and good intentions. But without sustainable support systems in place, you are building on sand.

Spend time putting in the wiring. Plan the plumbing. Install the HVAC system correctly. Assemble the invisible infrastructure that supports everything else.

Then leave it alone and watch it operate without you.

That's when you can say you've created something that lasts.

CHAPTER 7

Adapting to Change Orders

There's no reason to limit yourself to a single direction when the world offers hundreds of possibilities.
—Zaha Hadid

The staircase cost $80,000 to build. It was big and beautiful, with a metal frame and a custom design, in a large house. The construction crew spent weeks getting it perfect.

Then the owner walked in, looked at it, and said, "I don't like it. I don't want it."

We were shocked. "Why? Everything is beautiful and good. Why don't you want it?"

He just didn't like it. He wanted it removed and rebuilt differently.

I reminded him of what I'd recommended at the beginning of the project. "Remember, I'd suggested that we do an interior architectural design so you could see everything before construction started. Based on that design, you could have decided if you liked the staircase or not. But you didn't want it."

He said he didn't care about the cost to remove the staircase. He just wanted it gone, which would cost another $5,000 for demolition. Then we had to build a new staircase. I don't even remember how much that one cost him, but it wasn't cheap.

If we'd had the interior design at the beginning, the client could have said no to the staircase, and it would have never been built. He wouldn't have had to spend $85,000 for nothing.

After all of this, I again suggested that we do interior design for the remainder of the project. He said, "No, I don't want interior design."

I said, "In that case, prepare to spend more and more money."

An interior design would have cost him around $30,000. But because he wanted to save that money, he wound up losing $85,000.

That's what change orders cost; not just money, but time, momentum, team morale, and sometimes trust between you and the people you're leading.

What Change Orders Actually Are

A change order may arise for a variety of reasons: the client changes their mind, new information comes to light, or something approved needs to be different.

In architecture, change orders are part of the job. You plan for them. You price them. You have processes to handle them. But that doesn't make them easy.

I had a project once where, during the design process, the owner sold the house. The new owner didn't want the design we'd already been working on. He changed the whole project.

The new owner was a flipper. He bought houses, made fast changes, added more square footage, and sold the properties quickly. He didn't want a modern house because it would cost him more money. The initial design was for a modern-style house, so we had to change it to a traditional style.

We had to change everything.

It should have cost him more, but I couldn't apply the amount of the previous owner's deposit to this project. I could account for only the time we'd spent measuring the existing building, even though everything else had to be done from scratch.

It affected the timeline significantly because we had already submitted the project for a plan check. We'd cleared several departments, and then had to change the whole project and go through the entire process again.

That's the reality of change orders. You don't just change one thing. You change everything that was built on top of that thing, every approval that referenced the old design, every calculation based on the old parameters, and every timeline that was based on the old plan.

When Vision Meets Reality

The hardest part of a change order isn't the technical work of redesigning. It's the psychological work of letting go.

You have a vision. You plan it carefully. You get everyone to buy into it. You start building. Then something shifts, and you have to adapt.

Some leaders fight this. They insist that the original plan was best and everyone should stick to it. They see change as failure.

That's like an architect insisting on building a modern house even after the client has sold the property to someone who wants a traditional home. You can be right about the design being better and completely wrong about what needs to happen.

As I've said before about opportunities, I apply the same principle to change orders. We find a way to make it work.

That doesn't mean I like change orders. That staircase project frustrated me because it was completely preventable. The client could have paid $30,000 to see the design before we built it. Instead, he paid $85,000 for something he wound up not wanting. However, providing this type of insight, especially with so much money at stake, shouldn't mean refusal to adjust.

Even when change is frustrating, even when it costs more than it should, and even when it undoes work we're proud of, we adapt. Because the goal isn't to build what we want. The goal is to build what serves the client.

Maintaining Standards While Everything Shifts

Even after the staircase disaster and losing $85,000, the client still didn't want to invest in interior design and visualization.

At the very least, we convinced him to allow us to do interior design for the new staircase, permitting him to see a 3D model of how it would look and decide what he wanted. From there, with the interior design in place, we were able to move forward much more easily, and the process was smoother.

Interior design is important for clients who struggle to visualize a space, imagine how a feature will fit into a room, or anticipate how they'll feel in the home.

But here's what I didn't tell that client: sometimes, if a customer won't approve interior design, we do it anyway. We create the design for ourselves but don't show it to them, since they haven't paid for it. We do it for our own benefit.

Even though it costs me money, I don't mind, because I want to have a complete picture. I want to see everything clearly so I know how to proceed with the construction.

I do it so that the people on my team who are involved in the project feel confident.

That's how you maintain standards during change. You don't compromise on what you need to do the work, even if the client won't pay for it. You protect your team from uncertainty by creating clarity, even when it costs you personally.

When everything changes, people need something solid to hold onto. For my team, that solid thing is knowing exactly what we're building. If we have clear 3D models, detailed plans, and complete visualization, they can work confidently even when a project is in flux.

If I sacrificed that clarity to save money, I'd pay for it in mistakes, rework, and delays. Better to spend my own money on design work than to spend everyone's time and energy on confusion.

The Team Conversation Nobody Wants to Have

Because we needed to adapt the modern house into a traditional style, I was forced to tell my crew that their work would be undone. We'd spent weeks on the modern design, and it was stunning; clean, innovative, and precisely what the original client had wanted. The whole team was very proud of it.

So, I had to break the news: we would need to scrap the modern design. I didn't sugarcoat it; I told them the truth. The original owner had sold the property, and the new owner had something entirely different in mind. We would need to start from scratch, but at least we would get to measure the property.

Then I told them that the new owner was a flipper with numerous projects. If we handled this one well by delivering quickly and effectively, he could become a regular client, giving us several projects every year. This proved true. He soon became one of our regular clients and even referred a number of customers to us.

But I didn't know that would happen when we made the change. I just knew we had a choice: we could be angry about the wasted work, or we could see it as an opportunity. The rest of the team looked to me for guidance. If I were bitter, they would be bitter. If I complained about the lost time, they would feel their work didn't matter. Instead, I treated it as the norm. Changes in architecture are normal, and we can adapt.

Your team looks to you for emotional guidance. If you treat change as a disaster, they will do the same. If you treat it as an interesting puzzle, they will follow your example.

What If You Refuse to Adapt?

The client who wouldn't pay for interior design but wasted $85,000 on an unwanted staircase exemplifies a mindset I often see in leaders. They know they should invest in planning, in understanding what they are building before they build it, but planning costs money, takes time, and involves paying for something before enjoying its benefits.

Thus, they bypass it and proceed directly to construction, assuming they can address problems as they arise. Then problems do arise—big, costly ones that could have been prevented for a fraction of the expense. That client spent $80,000 on the staircase, another $5,000 to remove it, and additional money to build a new one, all to avoid spending $30,000 on interior design that would have revealed the problem.

In leadership, this manifests when leaders refuse to develop their team and then wonder why costly mistakes occur. When they avoid articulating strategies, they become frustrated when people move in different directions. When they forgo creating systems, they end up doing everything themselves. Change costs money, but the cost of refusing to plan and adapt is far greater.

When Change Threatens the Whole Structure

The design shift from modern to traditional also required changing the foundation. The modern design had a raised foundation, requiring four stairs to enter the house, which looks sleek and contemporary. The traditional design, on the other hand, was completely different and had only one step up from the ground.

This kind of change tests whether you truly understand what you are developing. Some architects might have tried to retain the elevated foundation and simply change the style of everything on top of it. That would have been simpler, but it would have been incorrect. Different types of foundations adhere to specific rules. The way a traditional house sits on a lot differs from that of a modern house. Keeping the modern foundation while giving the rest of the house a traditional design would not have looked right. People might not pinpoint why, but they would sense something was off.

When major changes occur, you cannot adjust only the surface. You have to address how changes impact everything beneath: the foundation, structure, and systems all the way down. In business, this is similar to the difference between transformational change and surface-level change. Transformational change transforms foundational values, systems, and fundamental ways of operating. Surface-level change just gives old processes new names. Genuine change requires more effort and expense, but it is the only approach that delivers real results.

The Confidence Problem

The hardest part of change orders is not the technical process or the cost; it is maintaining confidence when the future is uncertain. In rebuilding the modern house into a traditional one, there were moments when it was unclear whether it would work. The timeline was compromised, the budget increased, approval processes had to start over, and the crew was losing work.

This is when leadership matters most, not when everything is running smoothly, but when your plan has collapsed, and you are deciding the next steps. I held the team's confidence by remaining confident myself; not false confidence, but genuine confidence grounded in past experience with overcoming difficult obstacles. I also provided clarity wherever I could. Even if the project as a whole was uncertain, the team knew what to do next. We might not have had the answers to design questions, but we knew the answers to measurement, detail, and price questions. Breaking uncertainty into actionable tasks makes it manageable.

When necessary, I even spent my own money to create clarity. We produced interior designs for our own reference. This wasn't about the design itself; it was about giving the team concrete points to work from when everything else was uncertain.

People cannot be expected to work effectively in chaos. Creating islands of certainty is essential in navigating change.

What Doesn't Change

What I learned from all of this is that standards don't change even when everything else does.

The modern house became traditional, but the quality stayed the same. Attention to corners, hallways, and walk flow didn't change. Commitment to thinking about the person who would live there didn't change. Requirements for beautiful drawings, even if the client might not understand them, didn't change.

When the staircase was rebuilt, the new one had to meet the same standards as the first. In fact, it had to meet higher standards, because we now knew what the client didn't like and could design around it.

That's what "maintaining structural integrity during change" actually means. It doesn't mean the structure stays the same. Obviously, it changes, but the principles underlying it, the standards that define quality, and the values that drive decisions, remain solid even when everything built on top of them must shift.

If you change your standards every time circumstances change, you don't have standards. You have preferences. And preferences aren't strong enough to build on.

The Change You Don't See Coming

Both the staircase and the modern-to-traditional house projects entailed changes we could see. The client told us what would need to be different. We understood what needed to happen, even if it would be expensive and difficult.

The harder changes are the ones you don't see coming: the permit process that suddenly adds new requirements, the soil test that reveals problems with the foundation, the city plan checker who decides to interpret codes differently than they did on your last project.

You can't plan for those. You can't prevent them. You can only build the capacity to adapt quickly when such events occur.

That's why I keep my team engaged in challenges, like the $100 wager, problem-solving side missions, and the constant practice of figuring things out. It's not just about solving today's problems. It's about building the muscle to handle tomorrow's unexpected changes.

When something shifts that we didn't anticipate, I don't want my team looking to me to fix it. I want them to think creatively about solutions, research options, and come to me with ideas rather than just problems.

That capability doesn't develop during calm times when everything goes according to plan. It develops during change orders, when plans fall apart, and you have to figure out what to do next.

The Client Who Learned

After we finished that second staircase, the one that replaced the $80,000 mistake, I talked to the client about the rest of the project.

I said, "We can keep doing this. You can keep refusing interior design and then changing things after we build them. Or we can invest in seeing what things will look like before we build them and save you money on changes."

He finally agreed, not to a full interior design—he wasn't ready to spend that much—but to 3D models for major elements before we built them.

That changed everything. The rest of the project went smoothly. There were fewer changes, less waste, and better results.

Sometimes people must learn through experience, feeling the consequences of doing things the wrong way before they can learn to do them correctly. This can be frustrating, but it's true. As a leader, you cannot force others to learn from someone else's mistakes. Often, people must make their own mistakes, observe the results, and adjust accordingly. Your role is to be present when they are ready to change, not to say, "I told you so," but to guide them with, "This is how it should be done."

The Opportunity Hidden in Disruption

Remember the flipper who bought the house and forced us to change everything from modern to traditional? The change that pushed our timeline back and made us start over? That client ended up bringing us more work than almost anyone else. He became a steady source of projects, referred other clients to us, and trusted us because we managed the change process so well.

Had I been dogmatic about the modern design, resented the change, or made him feel guilty for disrupting our work, I would have lost future business. Change orders are costly and difficult, but they are also tests. They reveal whether you are flexible or fragile, whether you value your ideas more than the client's needs, and whether you handle problems effectively or break under pressure. Pass those tests, and you not only survive transitional periods, but you also earn the trust that brings more opportunities.

The question is not whether change will happen. In building and leadership, change is constant. People change their minds, new information arises, and circumstances shift. The question is whether you can adapt without compromising integrity. Can you alter a design while maintaining your standards? Can you shift direction without losing sight of quality?

When you know how to balance these factors, change need not sabotage a project. In fact, it can strengthen it.

PART III

Finishing and Legacy

We've talked about planning, building foundations, framing structures, installing systems, and adapting to change. But there's one more critical phase in construction that most people overlook until it's too late—what happens when you're actually done building and need to deliver something complete and functional.

That's where we're going next.

CHAPTER 8

The Completed Structure: Delivering Your Vision

Elegance lies in simplicity.
—Leonardo da Vinci

The house was only 1,200 square feet, very small for a custom home in California, where people expect more space.

But when I designed it, I had one set of goals: design it so that nobody can tell it's 1,200 square feet, so that it feels welcoming and the owners feel free in the space.

Anyone who walks into that house thinks it's over 2,000 square feet. They can't believe it when you tell them the actual size. The space flows well, the ceilings are proportionate, and natural light enters exactly right. It feels much bigger than it is.

This is one of my favorite projects. To this day, when the subject of custom houses arises, I show everyone this house. Even though I have an 18,000-square-foot house in my portfolio, I show people the 1,200-square-foot one.

Why? Because in an 18,000-square-foot single-family house, you can do almost anything you want. You have virtually unlimited space to work with. However, 1,200 square feet is a much smaller space, making it more difficult to include everything a client wants.

But we managed it.

That's what completion really means, not just finishing something, but delivering on the promise you made at the beginning, the promise that a small house would feel like a proud house, a good house, an inviting house.

When you can deliver that, when the finished project does exactly what you envisioned it would do, that's when you know you've completed something.

The Phone Call

When the architectural part is done, sometimes I joke with the client. I call them and say, "You know, there is a problem right now. You have to have your money ready."

They panic a little. "What happened? Why? What's wrong?"

I tell them, "The construction will start soon. So you have to have your money ready."

Then, when they come to my office to pick up the design or make the construction agreement, they almost always bring a gift.

Because they are happy with the project.

Currently, in my office, I have over 50 bottles gifted to me by clients; wine, whiskey, special beverages from their countries, and expensive things they wanted me to have.

That's something I'm proud of: that people are satisfied with the projects I help them create. They're so excited about what we've created together that they want to celebrate before construction even starts.

Most architects hand over drawings as they would hand over legal documents or technical paperwork. "Here are your plans. Good luck with construction."

I hand over drawings like I'm handing over a vision of their future. "This is what your family's life will look like. This is where you'll have coffee in the morning. This is where your kids will do homework. This is where you'll host dinners with friends."

The gifts aren't about the paper. They're about the possibility.

When Clients Become Family

I've been in the U.S. for nine years. Most of my friends were previously my clients.

We became friends while working on projects, and we moved forward together in life.

I don't remember designing any house where I wasn't invited to the housewarming. In Armenia, we have a ceremony for this, like a grand opening for the home. Almost every time I'm there, people call me and say, "Come. We're opening our house. We're moving in. We're having a party for our new home."

And they always introduce me to people and say, "Gevorg's company designed my house," mentioning anything we did on their project.

That's something I'm very proud of as well.

Because it's more than just paperwork. From architectural design to coordination with city planning and permitting, the process takes a very long time. By the time we're done, we're not just "architect" and "client" anymore. We've been through something significant. We've solved problems together. We've made decisions together. We've turned dreams into something real.

So we usually become friends.

Some architects try to keep a professional distance. They don't want to get too close to clients because it complicates business relationships. But I think that's backwards.

The relationship is the business. If I'm designing someone's home, I need to understand how they live, what they value, and what makes them comfortable. I need to know them. And if I do my job right, they know I care about them and their family, not just my fee.

When they invite me to their housewarming party, introduce me to their friends, and refer their relatives to me, it's not just a bonus. It's proof that the project actually succeeded.

What Success Actually Looks Like

People ask me how I measure success. They expect me to talk about the awards, our four consecutive years as Glendale's Best Home Builder, or to talk about company growth, from $500 to twelve computers and a full team.

Those things matter. I'm proud of them. But they're not how I measure whether I've actually delivered on my vision.

I measure success by whether a 1,200-square-foot house makes people feel free; by whether clients bring me gifts when they pick up their plans; by whether they call me to come to their housewarming parties; and by whether we become friends.

I measure success by whether the person who will live in the house for the next 20 years can clean it easily because I minimized corners; by whether they can use every square foot they pay property taxes on because I omitted hallways; and by whether they can walk through the home smoothly because I thought about how they move.

I measure it by whether, 50 years from now, someone will look at a building I designed and say, "Wow, that's beautiful," rather than, "That's old. We should tear it down."

Success in architecture isn't about the day you hand over the keys. It's about whether what you built serves people well for decades.

The same is true for leadership.

When Leadership Is Complete

In leadership, I never call anything complete. There is always something to grow.

But I count it as a success when the people you supervise know what to do, when they know how you think, and start to think like you.

In this way, everyone on the team is a leader.

You can consider your leadership successful because you now have a team of leaders. That's the greatest thing.

Remember David and Eva, my managers? I taught them everything I know. Now they handle projects without me. They make decisions I would have made, but they're making them. They solve problems I would have solved, but they're solving them.

That's completion in leadership. The work is never done, but core competencies have been transferred. The vision has been shared. The standards have been internalized.

When I started NextGen Vision with $500, I was the only person who could do anything. I was the architect, the project manager, the quality checker, and the client relationship manager. I did everything. The company could only grow to the extent I could personally handle.

Now? The company runs when I'm not there. Projects move forward when I'm traveling. Decisions get made when I'm unavailable. Quality stays consistent whether I'm reviewing the work or not.

That's not because I've finished building the company. It's because I've succeeded at building leaders instead of followers.

The building is never complete. But the structure is sound enough to keep growing without me holding every piece in place.

The Vision of the Next Generation

Why did I call my company NextGen Vision?

Everything we have today was once a vision of previous generations. NextGen Vision represents the vision of the next generation. We're not just building for ourselves; we're building for those who come after us.

I always strive to incorporate the latest, most modern designs and technologies into my business. That way, even 50 years from now, what we've built won't be considered outdated or in need of replacement. I want people to look at it and say, "Wow, that's beautiful."

That's the most important thing.

I want everyone to remember that Gevorg Grigoryan built something beautiful, even 50 or 100 years from now. I don't want my buildings to be torn down and replaced. Unless there's a disaster, they should still be standing, serving families, and remaining beautiful.

Most architects design for now. They follow current trends. They build what's popular today. In 20 years, those buildings will look dated. In 50 years, they will be torn down.

I'm designing for 100 years from now. That means I can't just follow trends. I have to understand what's timeless, what makes a space feel good regardless of what year it is, and what proportions work best for human beings, not just what happens to be in style.

The 1,200-square-foot house will still feel spacious in 2075. The flow will still work. The light will still be beautiful. Those things aren't about trends. They're about understanding how people live.

That's what I want my legacy to be—not that I built many buildings, and not that I won awards, but that I built beautiful things that lasted, that I created spaces where families thrived for generations, and that I taught a team who could keep doing the same after I'm gone.

The Ceremony That Matters

In construction, there's often a completion ceremony to commemorate the final inspection, certificate of occupancy, ribbon cutting, and the official handoff.

These moments matter. They mark the transition from construction site to finished building. They're important.

However, the real completion ceremony happens later. It's the housewarming party after the family has moved in, when their furniture is in place, when their kids are running through the rooms, when they're cooking in the kitchen, and hosting friends in the living room.

That's when you see whether the design actually works, whether the space serves the life they want to live, and whether what you envisioned on paper translates to comfort and joy in reality.

When I get invited to those parties, when I walk through a house I designed and see a family actually living in it, using it, and loving it, *that's* the completion that matters.

In leadership, the completion ceremony is even less obvious. There's no ribbon-cutting when someone you trained becomes capable of leading without you. There's no certificate when your team becomes a team of leaders.

But there are moments when you see it: when someone solves a problem you didn't even know about until after it was fixed; when the team handles a difficult client situation, and you only learn about it later because they resolved it; when someone you hired and trained three years ago is now training someone new, passing on what you taught them.

Those are the completion ceremonies for leadership, the quiet moments when you realize the structure you built is standing, growing, and succeeding independently.

What Gets Handed Over

When I hand over architectural drawings to a client, I'm not just giving them pieces of paper. I'm giving them blueprints for their future. Every line on those drawings represents a decision we made together about how they want to live.

When I finish a completed building for a family, I'm not just giving them the keys. I'm giving them a space that will hold their memories, support their daily life, and serve them for decades.

When I transfer leadership to the team I've trained, I'm not just delegating tasks. I'm giving them the capability to create, solve, build, and lead others as I led them.

That's what delivery actually means, not finishing something and walking away, but creating something that continues without you, that serves people long after you're gone, that improves over time rather than deteriorating.

The 1,200-square-foot house doesn't need me anymore. It's doing its job, making a family feel free and welcome in a small space. The building doesn't care that I designed it. It just works.

NextGen Vision no longer requires me to review every drawing. The systems work. The standards hold. The team leads. The company serves clients well, whether I'm in the office or not.

That's completion. It's not the end but the beginning of something that will outlast you.

Measuring What Matters

I could measure my success by square footage designed, number of projects completed, revenue generated, and awards won.

Those numbers would look good. They'd be easy to compare to those of other architects. They'd prove I've been successful by conventional standards.

But they wouldn't tell you whether I actually delivered on my vision.

My vision was never to design the most buildings. It was to design beautiful buildings that serve people well for generations.

My vision was never to run the biggest architectural firm. It was to build a team of leaders who care about quality as much as I do.

My vision was never to make the most money. It was to create work that makes me feel proud and to help clients create spaces they love.

So I measure success differently. I measure it by how many clients become my friends; by how many housewarmings I get invited to; by how many gifts of gratitude sit on my shelves; and by whether people still think my buildings are beautiful decades after I designed them.

I measure it by whether my team can solve problems without me; by whether they think about corners, hallways, and walk flow the way I do; and by whether they're becoming leaders, not just following my leadership.

I measure it by whether I'm building the next generation's vision, not just my own.

Those measurements are harder to quantify. They don't fit on a spreadsheet. But they're what actually matters.

The Building That's Never Done

Completion means the building is finished. You can point to a specific day when construction ends and occupation begins. There's a clear before and after.

But the work of architecture is never finished. The building will need maintenance, updates as needs change, and repairs over decades of use.

The good buildings adapt. They serve new and evolving purposes. They welcome new families. They last.

The bad buildings get torn down and replaced.

Leadership is the same. You can point to specific accomplishments: the team you built, the systems you created, the people you trained, and the problems you solved.

But the work of leadership is never finished. There's always more to learn, always another challenge, and always room to grow.

I never call anything complete because there is always something to grow.

The goal isn't to finish and be done. The goal is to build something strong enough to keep growing without you.

That 1,200-square-foot house? I finished designing it years ago. But it's still working, still making people feel free in a small space, still beautiful, and still serving its purpose.

NextGen Vision? I started it with $500 eight years ago, but it's not done. It's still growing, still serving clients, still building beautiful things, and still creating the next generation's vision.

In leadership, that's what delivering on your vision really means, not completing the work so you can walk away, but building something that continues the work after you've moved on to your next chapter.

The best buildings don't need their architect to keep functioning. They just work.

The best teams don't need their leader to keep succeeding. They just lead.

When you can hand over something that works without you, that grows without you, that serves its purpose without you, that's when you've truly delivered on your vision; not because you're done, but because what you've built is strong enough to stand on its own.

Then you get to do it again, build something new, solve a different problem, and create the next vision.

That's the real completion ceremony; not the end of the work, but the beginning of what comes next.

CHAPTER 9

Blueprints for Others: Teaching Your Architectural Approach

My work brings me joy, so I have no desire to leave it behind. —**Richard Rogers**

I don't look at resumes. I don't check portfolios. I don't call references.

When someone interviews at NextGen Vision, I ignore all of that.

Why? Because nobody is as perfect in their life as they are on their CV.

I know this because I used to provide my CV when I was looking for work. I know how people make themselves look better on paper than they are in reality. I know that friends will say nice things about you if you ask them for references. I know that portfolios show the best work, not the typical work.

So I don't look at any of it. Instead, I talk to the person, not professionally, but as I would a friend.

If the person being interviewed views the interviewer as a friend, they tend to be much more honest. The more honest they are, the better their chances of being hired.

I'm not looking at their professional skills because I can teach them what they need to know. I'm looking at how honest they are with me and whether they love architecture.

That's all I need to know. If the person is honest and loves architecture, I can teach them. If they don't love it, it doesn't matter how skilled they are or how impressive their resume looks. I will not be able to teach them.

You have to love architecture. That's the first tenet of being able to teach others.

What You Can and Cannot Teach

One time, a man came to my office. He had no experience or education in architecture. His background was in business management, but he wanted to be an architect.

I asked, "Do you really, really want this?"

He said, "Yes."

I told him, "Okay, if you love architecture, even if you don't know anything, I will teach you. Don't worry. But if you don't love architecture as much as you say, it doesn't matter how much you want it. I will not be able to teach you."

He loved it. So I taught him. He became a good architect.

But there was also a woman who came to my office with her father, who asked if we could hire his daughter. The woman told me she loved architecture and wanted to learn.

So we hired her. David and the other managers spent time teaching her. I also spent time with her.

But whenever we looked at her computer, she was either on Instagram or Facebook, scrolling through social media or shopping online. I could see that she didn't love architecture. She just wanted the job because she saw that architects sometimes become very famous, that they do beautiful jobs, and have proud moments.

But she didn't love the work itself.

After trying, we saw that she didn't want to learn. She wanted to accomplish big things, but had no real passion for architecture, and that's not what we want.

So I called her and said, "Sorry, but since you don't love architecture, I don't believe that you will learn it, and I don't believe you need to spend more time on it. Life is short. Find something you love, and go learn it."

She had been with us for two or three weeks. I thought maybe the money would inspire her, but I could see that nothing inspired her. She just didn't love architecture.

That's the lesson I learned from experience. You can teach skills. You can teach techniques. You can teach how to think about design, how to solve problems, and how to work with clients.

But you cannot teach someone to love what they're doing. They either love it or they don't. And if they don't love it, no amount of teaching will make them good at it.

Combining Two Educations

I went to architecture school in Armenia. My team in California learned architecture in the United States. Those are two very different forms of education, and I combine them both.

In Armenia, the climate is similar to that of Europe, with harsh winters and very hot summers. So our homes must be designed to be comfortable in any weather, which requires careful consideration.

Here in California, the weather is perfect. You can do almost anything design-wise. When you study architecture here, you rarely have to think about energy conservation based on outdoor temperatures or similar concerns.

But in Armenia, we think about it constantly.

Here, people learn about modern technologies that aren't so common in Armenia, mainly because construction materials differ. In California, we build everything from wood, while in Armenia, we use concrete. Implementing new technologies with concrete is much more expensive, so not everyone does it. Here, the walls are hollow, allowing for more flexibility. You can do almost anything you want.

I combine both approaches. We consider energy conservation; for example, bedrooms should be on the east-facing side of the house, and the living room should be on the west-facing side. Why? Because the sun rises in the east, so when you wake up, the morning sun naturally lights your bedroom, saving energy. In the evening, the sun sets in the west, filling your living room with light so you don't need to turn on the lights, saving energy again. This is something we focus on in Armenia, but it's less emphasized here, so I blend both perspectives.

To me, teaching isn't just about passing on a single way of doing things. It's about providing multiple perspectives: the Armenian approach and the American approach; the focus on energy efficiency and the focus on modern technology; the constraints of a harsh climate and the freedom of a mild one.

When you teach someone only one way, their approach is too limited. When you teach them multiple ways, they develop the ability to choose what's best suited to the situation.

The Moment Someone Becomes a Leader

David had been working in our office for just a couple of months. He was a drafter, a diligent worker, and learned quickly.

We already had two managers, so I wasn't even thinking about onboarding another one.

But I love to stay ready for anything.

One day, David came into my office and said, "You know, I have a friend who wants to work with us."

I said, "No problem. We can hire him, but under one condition: I don't have time to teach him anything. The other two managers don't have time either. Are you ready to teach him?"

He was surprised. "How can I teach him? I'm still learning. I don't know what to tell him."

I said, "He's your friend, and you seem happy here. Do you want him to work here and make more money? You can stand beside him as a friend and teach him."

He said, "Okay, I'm going to do that. I'm going to try it."

I explained to him, "As soon as you teach him, and he's able to start working, we'll put him on the payroll. Teaching is a process, and people usually pay to learn new skills. We don't charge for training, but trainees aren't paid during that time because it's like being in school."

I saw that David was ready, even though he was very young, just 22 or 23 years old at the time.

He took the responsibility, and I was very proud of him.

He taught his friend. Sometimes they had questions, and that's okay. They could ask the other managers, but the main point for me was that he took the responsibility.

That's one of the key points I look for when deciding whether someone can become a leader: not whether they know everything, not whether they're the most skilled, but whether they can take responsibility.

Can they see what needs to be done and do it, even if it's difficult? Can they teach someone else, even when they're still learning? Can they care about someone else's success as much as their own?

David was 22, and he could do that. That's when I knew he was ready to be a manager.

The Research Test

Another indicator that someone is ready to become a leader is how they handle questions.

When somebody comes to my office and asks me a question, and I have already answered that same question, I tell them, "You know the answer. Go find it."

I could think about it in terms of money. Since I pay hourly, I could consider my own interests and give them the answer immediately, saving the cost of the time they spend looking for the answer.

But I don't answer.

It's better for me to invest that money by giving them as much time as they need to learn the job more.

If they do the research and find the answers themselves, they are that much closer to leadership readiness. They learn more effectively than if I were to give them the answers.

Because if I give them the answers, they will always think, "Okay, Gevorg is right there. I can go and ask him."

But when they do their research, they will remember the answer forever.

This frustrates some people. They think I'm being difficult or that I don't want to help them. They don't understand that encouraging them to find the answer is a way of helping them.

Those who understand this, who accept the challenge and conduct the research, are the ones who become leaders because they've learned that they don't need me. They've learned that they can figure things out on their own.

Teaching Without Teaching

Here's the truth about how I teach people to think architecturally, to care about corners, hallways, walk flow, and all the things that make for great design.

I don't teach it.

I just do it and lead by example.

The first person who came to work for me observed how I work, what I look at, and she began to do the same. Then came the second person, who saw how we both did it, and they started doing it that way too. And so forth.

Everyone started to think the same way.

It's like parents with their children. You have to *be* what you wish to teach them. They are going to learn from you more than anyone else.

Be the person that you want each team member to be, and they will become that person.

Be disciplined, punctual, and friendly, and they will learn those things from you.

Be a leader, not a boss.

If you act like a boss, your team will resent you, and they won't learn from you. But if you lead by example, they'll start to respect and even admire you, wanting to follow your example because they see you as a good person.

You don't need to teach them anything beyond professional skills. You don't need to lecture them about caring for the people who will live in the homes you design. Instead, show that you care. Make it visible in your actions. You don't have to tell them to consider things like corners and dust; just consistently point out these details in every drawing you review, until your team members begin to notice and consider them on their own.

You don't need to teach them to take responsibility for mistakes. You just have to take responsibility for your own mistakes, every time, so that they can see you doing it.

They will copy not what you say, but what you do.

That's the most effective teaching method.

When the System Teaches Itself

Currently, if someone wants to join our team, I consult with Eva, David, and even the other workers, not just the managers. I specifically assess who has the time to teach a new hire.

"Okay, this guy has the time to teach someone new. This person will be their teacher."

I don't remember the last time I taught someone, maybe three or four years ago, because now I have a team of leaders who are capable of the task. Every single person in my office is a leader.

I no longer need to teach anyone. My team does the teaching. They are the people newcomers want to emulate. Training goes smoothly, and everyone is happy.

This is what successful teaching looks like. You don't continue teaching everyone indefinitely, but instead create a system in which people teach each other. The culture sustains itself, with new team members learning from those who came before them, who in turn learned from you.

The teaching has scaled beyond you.

When Eva teaches someone, she teaches them the way I taught her. That person teaches the next person the way Eva taught them, which is the way I taught Eva. The approach continues; the standards continue; the way of thinking continues, but it's no longer dependent on me.

That's the goal, not to be the only teacher, but to create teachers who create teachers who create teachers.

Happiness on the Job Site

Happiness on the job is the most important factor.

When you feel happy at work, it's not a job. It's something fun to do, like a hobby. It feels like visiting family.

That's what I'm actually teaching, not just how to draw plans, calculate loads, or deal with plan checkers. I'm teaching people that work can feel like this, that you can build a place people want to be, where people care about each other and grow together.

After hiring the woman who didn't love architecture, I could have kept her on the team. She could draw. She had basic technical skills. She could produce work that met minimum standards.

But she would have changed the culture. Her lack of love for the work would have been obvious. Others would have seen that you could work for my firm without caring about the work. The standards would have lowered.

So I let her go and told her to find something she loves.

Because the real teaching isn't about architecture. It's about showing people that when you love what you do, when you work with people you care about, when you take responsibility and help each other grow, work is merely an extension of life.

The Blueprints You Leave Behind

In architecture, blueprints communicate your vision to the people who will build it. They provide clear, detailed instructions that someone else can follow to create what you imagined.

In leadership, the blueprints you leave behind are the people you've taught. They are the instructions for how to keep building after you're gone.

When I started NextGen Vision with $500, I was the only blueprint. Everything was in my head. If something had happened to me, the company would have stopped.

Now? I haven't directly taught anyone in three or four years. The company has grown. The quality has stayed high. New people continue to join, learn, and become leaders.

That's because the blueprints I created (the people I taught, who taught others, who taught others) are now creating their own blueprints. David teaches people who teach people. Eva teaches people who teach people. Someone who started last year is already helping a person who started this month.

The architecture of leadership isn't about you being a great leader. It's about you creating more leaders, not followers who need you, but leaders who can stand on their own and create more leaders.

That's how buildings outlast their architects. The architect designs it, but the building serves people for generations after the architect is gone. The design is good enough to function without the architect.

Leadership is the same. If what you've built only works while you're actively building it, you haven't built anything. You've just been holding pieces together with your own hands.

But if what you've built keeps working, growing, and serving its purpose after you've moved on to the next thing, you'll know you've built something substantial that can endure on its own.

From Cleaner to Leader

Every single person in my office is a leader, from the janitor to the supervisor or manager.

Some people might laugh at that. "The janitor is a leader? What does that even mean?"

For example, when a new person joins the team and doesn't know where supplies are stored, the janitor can show them. When someone makes a mess, the janitor doesn't complain to management; they talk to the person directly about being more careful. The janitor takes responsibility for their role in making the office work, helps others when they can, and sets an example of doing good work.

Leadership is not defined by a particular job title or exerting authority over others, but by taking responsibility, helping others, and being the kind of person people want to work with.

When everyone in your organization is a leader, in that sense, you don't need much management. People see what needs to be done, and they do it. They help each other. They solve problems together. They teach each other.

Your organization becomes resilient. It can handle change. It can grow. It can adapt because it's not dependent on a single person or a small group to make everything happen.

That's the ultimate teaching, not to create people who are good at following your instructions, but to create people who can lead in their own way, in their own specialized area, for their own reasons.

What Architecture Schools Don't Teach

Architecture schools teach how to design buildings. They teach about structures, materials, codes, history, and theory.

But they don't teach you to think about the person who will clean the house you're designing. They don't teach you to minimize corners because corners are homes for dust. They don't teach you that hallways are wasted space that people pay property taxes on but don't use.

They don't teach you not to compromise on quality, even when the contractor wants to take shortcuts, because your name is the most important thing in this business.

They don't teach you that plans need to be beautiful, even if the client doesn't understand them, because that's how you earn the respect of other architects.

They don't teach you that the best way to lead a team is to take responsibility and give credit; that you grow your team, not just yourself; and that everyone should be a leader, not just the managers.

Those are the things I teach, not in place of the technical skills, but alongside them. Technical skills without the right mindset produce mediocre architects, and mediocre architects create buildings that are torn down in 50 years instead of buildings that people still call beautiful a 100 years later.

The Next Generation's Vision

We are not building our vision, but the vision of the next generation.

That's why I keep up with new, modern approaches to work, so that what I have built won't ever seem dated, so that no one will ever think it should be razed and rebuilt.

I want everyone to remember that Gevorg Grigoryan built something beautiful, even 100 years from now.

Teaching is the same. I don't teach people to do things my way. I teach them to think forward, to design for the next generation, to build things that endure, and to create beauty that outlasts trends.

When David teaches someone, he's not teaching them to copy me mindlessly. He's teaching them to think architecturally, to solve problems creatively, to care about quality, and to take responsibility.

When that person teaches the next person, the same process continues while adapting to new circumstances, technologies, and challenges.

That's how teaching outlasts the teacher. Specific techniques might change, but certain ways of thinking, high standards, and care for the work persist.

Your Blueprint for Teaching

If you want to teach others to become leaders, use what I've learned:

First, make sure people love the work. You can't teach someone to love something. They either do or don't. If they don't love it, help them find something else. Life is too short to spend it on work they don't care about.

Second, be what you want them to become. Don't lecture. Don't make rules. Just consistently be the kind of person you want them to be, where they can see you doing it. They will emulate you.

Third, encourage them to find answers. When someone asks you about something they should be able to figure out on their own, don't give them the answer. Make them research it. They'll remember forever what they discover for themselves.

Fourth, assess a person's responsibility, not their knowledge. A person willing to take the responsibility of teaching someone else, even while they're still learning, is your next leader.

Fifth, create teachers, not followers. Your job isn't to teach everyone yourself. Your job is to teach people who will teach people who will teach people. If you're still teaching everyone after several years, you haven't taught them effectively.

Sixth, everyone should be a leader, not just managers. Everyone should take responsibility, help others, and set an example. That's when your organization becomes strong.

Finally, build for the next generation. Teach people to think forward, to create things that will last, to build the future they want to see.

When you do all of this, you're not just teaching skills. You're creating a culture that perpetuates itself, a system that teaches itself, and a structure that keeps growing without you.

That's when your teaching has succeeded, not when everyone needs you, but when no one does, because you taught them so well that they became the teachers.

CHAPTER 10

The Song of Leadership

Architecture should do more than provide shelter; it ought to stir emotion, offer peace, and spark thought.
—Zaha Hadid

I wrote a song called "The Architecture of Leadership."

I'm not a musician, but sometimes words on paper aren't enough to capture what you're trying to say. Sometimes you need rhythm, metaphor, and poetry, something that hits differently than explanations and instructions.

I wrote this song to express what I've learned about leadership through building. I wanted something people can feel, not a lecture or manual, but something that captures the struggle, the vision, the cost, and the soul of actually building something that endures.

The Song

[Verse]
Bricks laid sturdy, mortar in the veins,
Foundation thicker than ancestral chains.

Columns rise steady, shoulders bear the weight,
Blueprints inked in sweat, leaders legislate.
Windows to the future, but the glass ain't clean,
Drafts blow through cracks where ambition leans.

[Chorus]
The architecture of the leadership,
Built on dreams and battleships.
Skyscrapers in the mind, reaching the zenith,
Blueprint of kings, believe it, achieve it.

[Verse 2]
Stairs spiral upward, trials twist tight,
Handrails of wisdom, gripping through the night.
Chandeliers of vision illuminate the dark,
Rooms filled with echoes where revolutions spark.
No shortcuts in this labyrinth of halls,
Every cornerstone is a testament to falls.

[Chorus]
The architecture of the leadership,
Built on dreams and battleships.
Skyscrapers in the mind, reaching the zenith,
Blueprint of kings, believe it, achieve it.

[Bridge]
Elevators rise, but they come with a cost,
Each button pressed, a lesson from the lost.
Roof of resilience, weathered by the storm,
Leadership's a structure, but the soul keeps it warm.

[Chorus]
The architecture of the leadership,
Built on dreams and battleships.
Skyscrapers in the mind, reaching the zenith,
Blueprint of kings, believe it, achieve it.

Breaking Down the Song to Build Up Your Leadership

Every line in this song connects to something real, something I've experienced, and something I've learned. Let me walk you through it and show you what I was thinking when I wrote each part.

Bricks Laid Sturdy, Mortar in the Veins

Bricks laid sturdy, mortar in the veins / Foundation thicker than ancestral chains

When I started NextGen Vision with $500, I wasn't just starting a company. I was laying bricks. Each client was a brick. Each project was a brick. Each person I hired and trained was a brick.

The mortar between those bricks? That was the relationships, the trust, the shared commitment to quality, and the way we treated each other like family.

I wrote "mortar in the veins" because it's more than just work. It becomes part of you. The standards get into your blood. The care for quality becomes automatic, not something you have to think about.

That foundation is thicker than ancestral chains. I wrote that line thinking about what my father taught me, what I learned in Armenia, and what got passed down to me. But what I'm building now needs to be even stronger than what I inherited. It has to carry not just me but everyone who comes after me.

I laid every brick in those early years, thinking, "Will this hold weight 50 years from now? Will this support what we're building on top of it?"

That's the difference between going through the motions and building a sturdy foundation.

Columns Rise Steady, Shoulders Bear the Weight

Columns rise steady, shoulders bear the weight / Blueprints inked in sweat, leaders legislate

I know what it feels like to have blueprints inked in sweat and shoulders bearing weight.

When I first came to America, I was living in Fresno, working as an architect at an hourly rate. Then I decided to move to Los Angeles. I moved without a job and opened NextGen Vision.

But I wasn't alone. I was with my family: my parents, brother, and sister. I was the person who said, "Let's go to Los Angeles. Fresno is too small for me to grow. I will make it work. There won't be any problems."

But I didn't have a job and had just started a new company. It was tough. Five people, including me, depended on me, and the company was still in its early stages. There were days, and especially nights, when I couldn't sleep because I was worrying about my family and my parents. I didn't want my parents to have to work; I believed it was my responsibility to take care of them.

But giving up was never an option. Everyone knows that Gevorg never gives in. He always stands tall.

Even though there were nights when I couldn't sleep, I found strength in my prayers. But I never showed my concerns. I wanted everyone to trust that I was a leader, the same Gevorg who stands on his own two feet and carries the weight of responsibility.

During that time, I thought constantly about how to grow my business. The blueprint for my company was drawn in hard work and sweat, with my shoulders bearing the weight.

I realized that leaders legislate. When I say, "My name is worth more than anything else in the world," and refuse to let a contractor take shortcuts, I'm setting a standard. When I declare, "Every fight is mine," and protect my team from political battles, I'm establishing the rules for how we operate.

You create the rules that govern your organization.

Windows to the Future, But the Glass Ain't Clean

Windows to the future, but the glass ain't clean / Drafts blow through cracks where ambition leans

This line is inspired by those moments when I could see where I wanted to go, but I wasn't sure exactly how to get there. The view wasn't perfectly clear. There were smudges on the glass. There were distortions.

I could see the general shape of NextGen Vision becoming what it is now: awards, growth, and a team of leaders. But I couldn't see every detail of the path.

Those drafts blowing through the cracks represent the vulnerability that comes with ambition. The bigger your vision, the more opportunities for self-doubt. The more ambitious your plans, the more ways things can go wrong.

I felt those drafts blowing when I was printing plans at a copy shop because I couldn't afford a plotter; when I fired six employees in 15 minutes and worried I was destroying what I'd built; when a client wasted $85,000 because he wouldn't listen to my advice.

Those moments when you wonder if you're doing the right thing, if you're good enough, if this is all going to work, those are the drafts blowing.

But you keep the windows open anyway, because you need to see the future, even if the view isn't perfect.

The Architecture of the Leadership

The architecture of the leadership / Built on dreams and the battleships

This is the chorus, the main idea I kept coming back to. Leadership has architecture. It has structure. It has design principles. It has foundations, frameworks, and systems.

I wrote "built on dreams and battleships" because you need both. The dreams are the vision: the 1,200-square-foot house that feels like 2,000 square feet; the company that started with $500 and grew to 12 drafters and four consecutive awards; the idea that buildings should still be beautiful 100 years from now.

The battleships are the reality of the fight: the difficult clients and the plan checkers who make things difficult because they're competitors. They are the mistakes and failures: the $85,000 staircase that had to be demolished, or that building in Russia that collapsed because they skimped on the foundation.

Dreams without battleships are fantasies. Battleships without dreams are fights without purpose.

But when you build with both a vision of the future and a willingness to fight for it, that's when you create something real.

Skyscrapers in the Mind, Reaching the Zenith

Skyscrapers in the mind, reaching the zenith / Blueprint of kings, believe it, achieve it

When I wrote this, I was thinking about the difference between small thinking and big thinking. The skyscraper is the ambition.

There is no such thing as a "biggest" vision. There is always something bigger.

Initially, my vision was to establish a company. Then it was to grow the company. Then it was to be the largest company in Glendale.

I've promised every single employee of mine that one day they'll be chairpeople of NextGen Vision.

Because NextGen Vision will be big. It will have innumerable projects and team members. I tell my team, "You are going to oversee them. You are going to lead them. We will eventually have thousands of leaders, not just employees."

That's the skyscraper. It's not a building with a certain number of floors but a structure that keeps growing, keeps expanding, and keeps creating leaders who create leaders.

The zenith isn't a destination. It's a direction. You're always reaching higher because there's always another level to build.

Stairs Spiral Upward, Trials Twist Tight

Stairs spiral upward, trials twist tight / Handrails of wisdom, gripping through the night

I wrote these lines thinking about that $85,000 staircase that had to be torn out. Stairs are never simple in architecture or in leadership.

They spiral upward, so you're not climbing straight up. You're going around and around, sometimes feeling like you're going sideways when you're actually ascending. The modern house that became traditional, and the employee I almost fired but gave another chance, are good examples of setbacks that felt like failures but were actually teaching me something.

"Trials twist tight" because the path isn't easy. It's narrow, difficult, and requires careful navigation, like the sewer line under the foundation, the fill soil that required going much deeper, or the client who wouldn't pay for interior design and therefore wasted money.

But "handrails of wisdom" are what you cling to when it gets hard. My handrails are the principles I established based on the lessons I learned from my father, my education in Armenia, my mistakes, and the experience I've accumulated.

"Gripping through the night" means holding on when you can't see clearly, when you're not sure it's going to work, when the path forward is dark but you keep climbing anyway because you trust the handrails.

Chandeliers of Vision, Illuminate the Dark

Chandeliers of vision, illuminate the dark / Rooms filled with echoes where revolutions spark

I wrote this thinking about why I spend my own money on interior architectural designs that clients won't pay for. Vision is like a chandelier. It doesn't just light one spot. It spreads light across a whole room. When you have a clear vision, everyone can see clearly. Everyone knows where they're going and why it matters.

I keep that chandelier lit. I need my team to see clearly what we're building, even when circumstances are dark or uncertain.

"Rooms filled with echoes where revolutions spark" is about legacy. What you create continues to echo after you're done creating it. The people I teach go on to teach others. The buildings I design serve families for generations. The principles I establish continue to guide decisions long after I'm gone.

Revolutions spark in those rooms because when you change how people think, when you show them a better way, it spreads. David teaches his friend, who then teaches someone else, who then teaches someone else; that's a revolution, a change in how things are done that keeps propagating outward.

I haven't taught anyone directly in three or four years, but the teaching continues because the revolution sparked.

No Shortcuts in this Labyrinth of Halls

No shortcuts in this labyrinth of halls / Every cornerstone a testament to falls

I hate hallways because they're wasted space. But when I wrote this line, I was thinking about how, in leadership, the difficult paths, the indirect routes, and the long way around are necessary.

"No shortcuts" means you can't skip the foundation work. You can't avoid teaching people properly. You can't take the easy way just because the right way is more challenging.

I wrote this thinking about that building in Russia that collapsed. They tried to take shortcuts on the foundation. They tried to save money on the part nobody would see, and three stories came down.

"Every cornerstone a testament to falls" is possibly my favorite line in the whole song. The cornerstones, the critical pieces that hold everything together, are made from failures, what you learned when things didn't work.

I learned about the importance of interior design from that $85,000 staircase disaster. I learned about protecting team culture from having to fire six people at once. I learned about the price of integrity from people who disrespect their work by charging too little.

Those falls became cornerstones. Those failures became the foundation for better decisions later.

Elevators Rise, But They Come With a Cost

Elevators rise, but they come with a cost / Each button pressed, a lesson from the lost

This is the song's bridge, and it's the key metaphor I wanted to explore: elevators versus stairs.

I started from the bottom.

I didn't work solely for architectural firms. I also worked as a hookah server, similar to a waiter, and I always understood how employees felt about their bosses. Later, I became a manager and learned what it means to lead a team and interact with both employees and supervisors.

After coming to America, I worked as a drafter, not yet as an architect, and then as a city expediter, handling permits by working with city officials.

Then I opened my company.

I learned everything from the ground up—every story, every challenge, at every level. When I founded my company, I assumed every role myself. So, when I began hiring people, I already understood that if I acted like a certain kind of boss, people wouldn't like me; they'd end up resenting me.

If you take the elevator, meaning shortcuts, you might reach the top quickly, but you'll never understand what it feels like to experience the first, second, third, fourth, and all the other floors along the way. You'll be at the top, but your team will resent you. They'll sit at their computers and do the bare minimum, caring only about their paycheck, not about your business.

But if you've experienced every step yourself, you know what it takes to be a good leader. You care for your business and your people, and in turn, they respect you and feel invested in your success. They see your business as their own.

That's the cost of taking shortcuts. If you end up at the top without truly understanding the journey, you'll miss out on genuine connection and support. As a result, no one will truly take care of your business, and you'll risk losing both your company and your customers' trust.

Roof of Resilience, Weathered by the Storm

Roof of resilience, weathered by the storm / Leadership's a structure, but the soul keeps it warm

I wrote this verse thinking about how you build the roof after everything else is in place. Foundation, framing, systems, walls, and finishes are completed first, followed by the roof. It's the last major structure, and it's the one that must withstand everything that comes from above it.

Resilience isn't something you can install at the beginning. It's what you develop after being tested, after the storms hit, things go wrong, and you have to keep going.

My roof of resilience was built storm by storm: the clients who changed everything mid-project; the plan checkers who made things difficult; the employees who didn't work out; the projects that cost more than expected; the setbacks, complications, and unexpected problems.

The roof weathered each storm, but each storm made it stronger, proving it could hold.

Then there's the last line: "Leadership's a structure, but the soul keeps it warm."

This is what I really wanted to say with the whole song.

You can have a perfect structure with a perfect foundation, framing, and systems, but if there's no soul, it's just a building. It's not a home.

The soul is the care, the love for the work, the commitment to family culture, the protection of my team, the refusal to compromise on what matters, the joy in seeing someone learn, and the pride in creating something beautiful.

The soul of NextGen Vision is in the morning coffee conversations, and in the way we say "you are never wrong" when someone makes a mistake. It's in the way David took the responsibility to teach his friend the job when he was only 22 years old. It's in the way I do interior designs on my own dime, so the team can have clarity. It's in the way I confronted a valuable client who had disrespected a young woman on my team.

That's what keeps the structure warm. That's what makes it livable. That's what makes people want to be there.

The soul of NextGen Vision became clear to me one day.

I went to the office to do some work and saw that the door was already open. I thought maybe I had forgotten to close the door or that one of my employees had forgotten to close it. It was a Sunday.

I entered and saw my team.

I said, "What are you doing here? We don't have any projects. We are not behind on any timelines."

They said, "We are here just to drink a coffee together. Just to talk a little bit."

That's the soul. That's the family atmosphere in the office. They want to be there because it's a warm place for them to be together.

I said, "Why didn't you call me so that I could join you?"

The person who arranged it was very young and a little shy. I said, "Never be shy. I'm your brother. I'm not a stranger. At work, I might be the owner of the business. Eva and David might be your managers. But outside of work, we are all brothers and sisters."

That's the soul of the company: when people choose to come to the office on a Sunday, not because they have to, but because they want to be together; when the structure feels warm enough that it becomes home.

Without soul, you just have an efficient machine. With soul, you have a family that also happens to do great work together.

Why I Wrote This Song

I wrote this song because I realized that everything I'd learned about architecture applies to leadership, not merely as loose metaphors but as structural principles.

You really do need a foundation in leadership, and it must be sufficiently robust to bear weight.

You really do need columns to distribute the load across multiple people.

You really do need windows so people can see the future.

You really do need stairs so people can climb, even if it's more challenging than using the elevator.

You really do need a roof to weather the storms.

And you really do need a soul to keep it all warm.

The song helped me see these connections clearly. Writing it forced me to think through what I actually believe about how to build something that lasts.

I wanted to share it because it may help you see the connections as well. The metaphors may stick in your mind in a way that explanations wouldn't. Maybe when you're facing a difficult decision, you'll remember "no shortcuts in this labyrinth of halls" and choose the more difficult but correct path.

Maybe when you're tempted to compromise on quality, you'll remember "leadership's a structure, but the soul keeps it warm" and realize that some things are worth protecting, even when they cost you.

The Rhythm and Flow of Great Leadership

Music has rhythm. Leadership does too.

There's the daily rhythm of morning coffee, project discussions, computer work, and problem solving.

There's the weekly rhythm of project reviews, team check-ins, and coordination meetings.

There's the monthly rhythm of new projects starting, permits coming through, construction projects finishing, and clients celebrating completions.

There's the yearly rhythm of hiring cycles, award seasons, strategic planning, and reflecting on growth.

And there's the long-term rhythm, the cycle of teaching someone who teaches someone who teaches someone; the cycle of building that is handed over, lived in, and lasts for generations.

When I wrote this song, I tried to capture that rhythm. The verses build, the chorus reinforces them, the bridge adds complexity, and it all flows together into something that feels complete.

Great leadership has that same flow. It's not jerky or inconsistent. It's smooth. People know what to expect. Systems work reliably. Standards stay consistent. Culture perpetuates naturally.

The song flows because the architecture is sound. Leadership flows because the structure is solid.

Your Song to Write

This song is mine. It captures my journey, my metaphors, and my way of seeing leadership through the lens of architecture.

But you need to write your own.

What are the metaphors that capture your leadership? What are the images that represent your values? What's the rhythm of how you work? What's the soul that keeps your structure warm?

Maybe your metaphors aren't about buildings. Maybe they're about gardens growing, ships sailing, or orchestras playing. Your metaphors can be whatever makes sense for your work and your way of seeing the world.

But find your song. Find a way to express what you're trying to build.

Because the song helps people understand. It helps them remember. It helps them feel what you're trying to create, not just think about it.

And when they understand and feel it, they can help you build it.

That's what this chapter is really about, not just my song, but the idea that leadership needs both sides: the practical structure and the artistic expression, the blueprint and the song, the architecture and the soul.

I built the structure across the preceding chapters: the foundations, the framing, the systems, the adaptation to change, the completion, and the teaching.

Then I wrote the song to capture the soul of it all, to express what it feels like, not just explain it.

When the structure is sound, and the song is beautiful; when the systems work, and the soul is warm—that's when you've created something that will last.

People will sing it, talk about it, and admire it, even after you're long gone.

That's the architecture of leadership.

Built on dreams and battleships.

Skyscrapers in the mind, reaching the zenith.

Blueprint of kings.

Believe it. Achieve it.

Conclusion

The present is the shifting line separating what has passed from what is ahead, and within that boundary sits hope. **—Frank Lloyd Wright**

The building is never finished.

I started NextGen Vision with $500 nine years ago. Today, we have 12 computers, 12 drafters, project managers, and a whole team. We've won Glendale's Best Home Builder four consecutive years. We've completed projects that families live in and love. We've created a culture where everyone, from the janitor to the supervisor, is a leader.

But I never call anything complete because there is always something to grow.

That's not a problem. That's the whole point.

When you think architecturally about leadership, you understand that completion isn't the goal. Quality is the goal. Growth is the goal. Legacy is the goal.

Buildings get finished. You hand over the keys. The family moves in. That project is complete.

But the work of architecture continues. You learn from what worked and what didn't. You apply those lessons to the next project. You develop your skills. You refine your approach. You keep building better and better versions of what you're capable of creating.

Leadership is exactly the same.

What You've Learned to Build

I've shown you how to think about leadership the way an architect thinks about buildings.

You've learned that vision needs to be clear enough for others to see it. You need blueprints, actual plans that people can follow. Foundations must be solid, built on principles you won't compromise, even when it costs you.

You've learned that a functional structure distributes weight among multiple people rather than burdening one person. Systems are the invisible infrastructure that makes everything else possible. Change is inevitable, and you must adapt without losing integrity.

You've learned that completion means creating something that works without you. Teaching means becoming the person you want others to be. Leadership has both structure and soul, and you need both.

But learning isn't the same as building.

Now you have to actually construct something.

Begin Your Vision Today

The first thing you have to do is dream. What do you want to become?

The second thing is to decide.

The third thing is to write. Design the path and how you want to achieve it. Then write down your plan. How will you move forward? What resources do you need to start?

The truth is, you don't need any resources. If you dream big enough, you can achieve it. You can start from zero, as I did.

Don't wait until you have resources. Don't wait until you have a team. Don't wait until circumstances are perfect.

I started with $500. That wasn't enough to buy a computer and a plotter. It was barely enough to register the company. But it was enough to start.

Your starting point might be even smaller than mine was. Maybe you're still in school. Maybe you're working for someone else. Maybe you don't have any money at all.

It doesn't matter. You can start building your leadership architecture today.

An architect examines a property and begins to imagine what could be on it.

Your property is the world. The whole world is your building site.

Imagine it, and dream big. Never settle for smaller. Small things are easy to achieve, and if you focus only on them, you'll lose your greater vision.

If you dream big, you'll keep challenging yourself. Your life will feel more interesting, like a good book you never have to put down.

The foundation work can begin anywhere. You can establish your principles, the non-negotiables that you'll never compromise on. You can decide what kind of leader you want to be. You can start treating people the way you'd treat them if you were already the leader you want to become.

You can practice thinking architecturally. When you see a building, think about why it was designed that way. What problems did the architect solve? How is the structure's weight distributed? How do the systems work together?

When you're part of a team, even if you're not leading it, you can observe the architecture. How does information flow? Where are the bottlenecks? What would you do differently? How would you structure this if you were designing it?

You're not waiting to become a leader. You're preparing to naturally step into that role when the opportunity comes.

The Building Never Ends

I've achieved things I could have never imagined when I started: awards, growth, recognition, and a team of leaders who can run everything without me.

But I'm not done and never will be.

Currently at NextGen Vision, we are evaluating new technology, implementing AI, and other innovative tools.

Always improve. Go along with the era in which you are living. Use everything to your advantage, not the people or the materialistic things, but the wisdom. Use everything that you can to achieve your dreams.

Don't wait for things to break before you improve them. When things are working well, that's the perfect time to make them work even better. When you're successful, that's when you prepare for the next level of success.

Continuous improvement doesn't mean you're always fixing problems. Sometimes it means you're making good things better. You're raising standards. You're expanding capability. You're preparing for challenges you have not yet faced.

The best time to strengthen your structure is when there's no storm. The best time to improve your systems is when they're working. The best time to develop your team is when everything is running smoothly.

Because storms will come. Change will happen. New challenges will emerge.

If you only improve when things are broken, you'll always fall behind. You'll always be reacting. You'll always be in crisis mode.

But if you improve continuously, when challenges arise, you'll be ready. You'll know your structure can handle the load. Your systems will be able to adapt. Your team will rise to the occasion.

The One Thing to Remember

If you forget everything else in this book, remember this:

Love whatever you do. If you love it, you will achieve it.

Your dreams should be based on your own passions, not on what others love. My dad loves being a lawyer, but that doesn't mean I should try to be the best lawyer in the world. If your neighbor loves being a doctor, your dream shouldn't be to become a doctor just to follow their passion.

Your dream should be what you love most.

Everything else flows from that. All the other principles, all the techniques, all the stories and examples, they're all built on top of that one foundation.

Get that right, and everything else becomes possible. Get that wrong, and nothing else will work, no matter how hard you try.

What I Wish Someone Had Told Me

When I started with $500, everything was good at that time. But when I began to hire people and grow the business, I wish someone had taught me how to lead.

It was my first time owning a company. I had previous experience as a manager and supervisor, but never as a founder.

When the first person I hired had questions, she came to me with them, and I said, "Oh, don't worry, I'll take care of it." When the second employee I hired approached me about an issue and said, "Oh, this doesn't work." I said, "Okay, don't worry. I'll handle it."

Never do that.

Teach them how to do it. Always teach your followers to be leaders. It will only make you stronger.

That's what I wish someone had told me from the beginning. Don't solve everyone's problems for them. Teach them to solve problems themselves. You're not helping them by doing everything; you're weakening both them and yourself.

I learned these things through experience, all the mistakes, setbacks, failures, and expensive lessons.

You don't have to learn everything the hard way. You can learn from others who've already paid the price for their knowledge.

But you will need to learn some lessons for yourself. That's okay. That's necessary. Remember what I wrote in the song: "Every cornerstone is a testament to falls."

Your failures will teach you things that success never could. Your mistakes will become the foundation for better decisions later.

Don't fear failure. Fear not learning from it.

Resources for Your Journey

History is crucial. Read about the great leaders of the world.

Alexander the Great was a good leader. Even Napoleon was a good leader.

Read about the most prominent world leaders. How did they do it?

Napoleon knew every single soldier by name. That's why his soldiers respected him. They regarded him as an older brother.

Know every single person who follows you by name. It doesn't matter how many people that might be.

Study history. Study great leaders, not to copy what they did, but to understand the principles underlying their success. Then apply those principles in your own way, in your own time, with your own vision.

We Are Building the Next Generation's Vision

Why did I call my company NextGen Vision?

Because everything we have today was once a vision of the previous generation. NextGen Vision is the next generation's vision. We are building the vision of the next generation.

That's what I want you to understand about legacy. You're not building for yourself. You're building for people who will come after you, people who don't exist yet; families who will live in the homes you design, team members who will learn from the leaders you develop, and organizations that will use the systems you create.

When you build with that mindset, everything changes. You can't take shortcuts because shortcuts will fail the next generation. You can't compromise on quality because quality has to last. You can't build just for now because you're building for the future.

Fifty to 100 years from now, I want people to look at what I built and say, "Wow, it's beautiful." I want to design buildings that don't get destroyed and replaced. I want to instill leadership principles that don't become outdated. I want to create an approach to work that people respect across generations.

That's possible. But only if you build with the next generation in mind.

Your First Blueprint

Right now, today, before you do anything else, draw your blueprint.

Not a perfect one. Not a complete one. Just the first draft.

What do you want to build? What principles will you refuse to compromise? What kind of leader do you want to become? What legacy do you want to leave?

Write it down. Draw it out. Make it concrete enough that someone else could look at it and understand what you're trying to create.

That blueprint will change. It will evolve as you learn. You'll revise it as circumstances shift. That's fine. That's expected.

But you need a starting point. You need to know what you're building toward so you can take the first step in that direction.

My first blueprint was simple: create an architectural firm where people feel like family, and we build beautiful things that last. That was enough to start with. Everything else developed from there.

Your first blueprint might be even simpler. That's okay. Simple is often better than complex when you're just beginning.

Draw it today.

The Architecture of Your Leadership

The building techniques I've shown you aren't just for architects. They're for anyone who wants to build something that matters.

Teachers build educational systems. Parents build family cultures. Managers build team capabilities. Entrepreneurs build companies. Anyone who wants to create something that will outlast them can benefit from the architecture of leadership.

You don't need to understand architecture to use these principles. You just need to think structurally about what you're building.

What's your foundation? What are your non-negotiables?

What's your framing? How are you distributing responsibility?

What are your systems? What infrastructure makes everything else possible?

How do you adapt to change without losing integrity?

What does completion look like? When have you successfully delivered on your vision?

How are you teaching others so your work continues without you?

These aren't just metaphors. They are the actual structural requirements for building leadership that endures.

The Soul That Keeps It Warm

Remember the last line of the song: "Leadership's a structure, but the soul keeps it warm."

Don't get so focused on architecture that you forget humanity. Don't build such perfect systems that you lose care for people. Don't create such efficient structures that you squeeze out the joy.

The soul is what makes people want to be there. The soul is what makes work feel like family. The soul is what makes your leadership worth following.

Structure without soul is just machinery. Soul without structure amounts to good intentions that never materialize into anything real.

You need both.

Build the structure carefully, thoughtfully, and soundly, but keep the soul alive in every decision, every interaction, and every moment.

That's what makes the difference between a building people have to use and a home people want to live in.

Begin

You have the blueprints now. You understand the principles. You've seen the examples. You know what works and what doesn't.

Now it's time to build.

Start small if you need to. I started with $500. You might start with even less. That's fine.

Start where you are. Don't wait for better circumstances, more resources, or clearer direction.

Start today. Draw your vision. Establish your principles. Take the first step toward becoming the leader you want to be.

And then keep building. Day by day. Brick by brick. Person by person. System by system.

The building never ends, but that's not a burden. It's an opportunity, an invitation to keep growing, keep improving, and keep creating something better.

Fifty years from now, 100 years from now, will people say, "Wow, that's beautiful," when they look at what you built?

That depends on what you start building today.

The architecture of your leadership is waiting to be designed.

The foundation is ready to be laid.

The blueprint is ready to be drawn.

Begin.

"Everything that we have today was once a vision of the previous generation.

What will be your vision for the next generation?"

www.ingramcontent.com/pod-product-compliance
Lightning Source LLC
Chambersburg PA
CBHW060536130626
46553CB00002B/786

* 9 7 9 8 8 9 5 7 6 1 7 4 8 *